A Study Guide to Mark's Gospel

A Study Guide to Mark's Gospel

Discovering Mark's Message for His Day and Ours

By
Scott Gambrill Sinclair

BIBAL Press
Publishing agency of BIBAL Corporation
Berkeley Institute of Biblical Archaeology and Literature

A Study Guide to Mark's Gospel
Discovering Mark's Message for His Day and Ours

Library of Congress Cataloging-in-Publication Data

Sinclair, Scott Gambrill.
    A study guide to Mark's Gospel : discovering Mark's message for his day and ours / by Scott Gambrill Sinclair.
        p.   cm.
    Includes bibliographical references.
    ISBN 0-941037-44-4 (pbk. : alk. paper)
    1. Bible. N.T. Mark—Study and teaching.   I. Title.
BS2585.5.S55 1996
226.3'077—dc20   96-35882
                                                            CIP

Published by BIBAL Press
P.O. Box 821653
N. Richland Hills, TX 76182

Cover by KC Scott, Ashfield, MA
Printed in the U.S.A.

In thanksgiving for

my brother Mark

and

the people of St. Mark's Episcopal Church

Berkeley, California

Contents

Contents

Preface

Some people read Mark's gospel primarily to learn what Jesus said and did. Since Mark's gospel is an early—indeed, the earliest—biography of Jesus, they turn to it to gain information about him.

For Christians, a presupposition of this approach to the gospel is that we come to know God by looking at the historical Jesus. Jesus was God incarnate, and thus to learn about God, we need to study what Jesus actually said and did.

Other people read Mark's gospel to stimulate subjective reflection. They go through the gospel, hoping that some image or phrase will "jump out" at them and lead to personal insights about their own lives and relationships to God.

For Christians, a presupposition of this approach is that the Holy Spirit guides our meditations as we interact with the Bible. When we read God's word, the Spirit helps us find special messages that address our unique situations and needs.

As a Christian, I myself hold both presuppositions and so read Mark in both ways. I believe that we do come to know God by looking at the historical Jesus and that the Holy Spirit does give us personal messages as we read the Bible. Hence, we should read Mark both to learn about what Jesus said and did and to promote subjective reflection.

There is, however, a third way to read Mark's gospel: One can read the gospel to discover what the evangelist was trying to say to the church of his own time. Like later Christian preachers and writers, Mark responded to specific problems in his day and retold the story of Jesus to address them. Therefore, his presentation about Jesus challenged his first readers to come to particular conclusions which would lead to certain choices. For more than half a century, many scholars have concentrated on reading Mark to discover what these conclusions and choices might have been.

For Christians, a presupposition for trying to discover Mark's specific message to his first readers might be that we learn about God primarily by looking at individuals whose actions have been shaped by their understanding of Jesus. God is especially visible in the lives of people who seek to know and obey Jesus. Mark was such a person, and by looking at how he retold the story of Jesus to address the needs of his own time, we can discover something about what God would say to us today.

Of course, discovering what Mark was trying to communicate to the people of his own time should help us both in learning about the historical Jesus and in using the Scripture for subjective reflection. If we know the "slant" Mark placed on his portrayal of Jesus, we can take that into account as we try to look behind the gospel to see Jesus himself. Similarly, if we know what Mark's point of view was, we can make that viewpoint itself a subject for personal reflection. Perhaps Mark's message to his original readers has a special application to our individual lives today.

In the following little book, I will concentrate on discovering what Mark was saying to the Christian readers of his own time. Specifically, we will go through the gospel section by section and see what Mark's primary points to his original audience were. To help us do this, I will first provide a new translation of a section. I hope that giving a new translation will help readers experience the sometimes all-too-familiar material in a fresh way. Then we will try to discover what the basic message of the section would have been for the first readers of the gospel. Of course, as we look at the messages of one passage after another, the message of the gospel as a whole will emerge.

By going through the gospel section by section and concentrating on the major points, we will experience the gospel much the way Mark's original audience did. Here we should note that

Mark's original audience was scarcely in a position to do detailed analysis. In an era when there were no Xerox machines, documents were always in short supply and the usual way that people encountered texts was by hearing them read. Hence, most Christians could not flip pages to remind themselves of what had been or would be covered, or even pause for careful study of the passage at hand. All a hearer could do would be to listen to the flow of the story, note the major emphases, and draw preliminary conclusions as the reading progressed.

To find Mark's message for the readers of his time, we will especially look at how Mark has arranged and worded his material and also examine any changes he seems to have made in its content. Before Mark wrote his gospel, people mostly repeated the individual traditions about Jesus by word of mouth. Naturally, under these circumstances the sayings of Jesus and the stories about him had no fixed order, since preachers and teachers varied the order depending on what points they were trying to make. Also, there must have been variations in wording, since we do not normally repeat oral material word for word. Hence, when Mark wrote his gospel, he had some freedom in how he organized the sayings and stories and in how he worded them. Not surprisingly, Mark used this freedom to help communicate his own concerns. Accordingly, by noticing how he arranged and worded material, we can get some idea of what those concerns were. Naturally, any changes Mark made in the tradition are especially informative concerning what he was trying to communicate. We must also assume that his original audience would have been at least fairly sensitive to how Mark arranged, worded, and altered stories, since his Christians hearers would already have been familiar with the individual stories and so would have noticed how Mark put his personal stamp on them.

To help modern readers reflect on whether Mark's message is helpful today, I will pose a couple of questions for reflection at the end of each section.

PREFACE

I have written this book primarily for lay people who want a very brief introduction to the gospel that will highlight its essential message and can be used for individual or group reflection. I originally prepared the translation and most of the commentary for an introductory course on Mark that I taught at Dominican College, San Rafael, California.

Biblical scholars will find much of the material familiar, but may be interested in my treatment of the socalled "messianic secret." For generations now, scholars have puzzled over why Jesus sometimes tries to hide his identity and miracles in Mark and yet at other times insists on proclaiming them. I have attempted here to give a coherent explanation which does justice to each instance, and I believe that in some respects it is original.

The rise of inclusive language provides a special challenge to the translator and commentator. In this book I have used inclusive language when referring to human beings. To make the language inclusive, I have adopted the colloquial usage of "they" and "them" to refer to "anyone" or any member of a class. I have followed Mark's usage in retaining masculine pronouns for God.

I gratefully acknowledge my indebtedness to many. The Rev. Lin Ludy read the initial draft, made helpful suggestions, and urged me to publish the book. The Rev. Ronald Culmer, Mrs. Jane Hartman, and Mrs. Ann Kurteff read later drafts and encouraged me. Ann also made many minor corrections. Dr. Duane Christensen persuaded me to turn the book into a study guide by including questions for reflection. The Rev. Robert Haberman read the final version and convinced me to add a few more such questions. Some of the ideas I offer here first appeared in a small article I published in *St. Luke's Journal of Theology* in 1990. At various points in my discussion of the miracles in Mark, I have taken over the ideas found in L. William Countryman, "How Many Baskets Full? Mark 8:14–21 and the Value of Miracles in Mark," *Catholic Biblical Quarterly*

47 (1985):643–55. In preparing my translation of Mark's gospel I made heavy use of Daryl D. Schmidt, *The Gospel of Mark with Introduction, Notes, and Original Text* (Sonoma, CA: Polbridge Press, 1991). On grammatical and textual matters I am especially indebted to Vincent Taylor's monumental *The Gospel According to St. Mark: The Greek Text with Introduction, Notes, and Indexes* (London: MacMillan, 1952). My own translation is based on the third edition of the United Bible Societies' Greek text. However, in some instances where I disagreed over what the original reading was, I translated something that appears only in the textual apparatus.

1. Mark 1:1

The beginning of the good news of Jesus the Messiah, God's Son (1:1).

In all probability, the opening phrase of Mark's gospel was originally its title. Since the phrase does not contain a verb, it could hardly have been the first sentence. The book's traditional title, "The Gospel According to Mark," presupposes a collection of "gospels." Mark is the earliest of these volumes, and so could not initially have had this label.

When Mark was writing, "gospel," the Greek word for *good news*, was already a shorthand designation for the Christian message as a whole. This usage is clearly present in Paul's letters (e.g., Rom 1:16), which antedate Mark's gospel by at least a decade. The same usage occurs in Mark itself (e.g., 13:10).

The title "The Beginning of the Good News of Jesus the Messiah, God's Son" especially alerted Mark's original readers to the fact that he would only narrate the first part of the Christian story. Consequently, this warning should have helped them cope with the disconcerting end of the book when the women flee from the empty tomb and say nothing to anyone.

The title also invites us to pay particular attention to the subsequent use of the descriptions "Messiah" [Christ] and "God's Son." As we shall see, these terms will be crucial in the narrative.

Within the early church for whom Mark was writing, the title Messiah especially suggested a king. Originally Messiah— or to use Mark's Greek term, "Christ"— meant anyone who was anointed. The Hebrew Scriptures (the Christian Old Testament) direct that anointing be used to install people into various important offices such as the priesthood (Exod 29:7). The "anointed," properly speaking, was the king of Israel or Judah (e.g., Ps 2:2). After the monarchy collapsed, the Hebrew

Scriptures and subsequent Jewish writings looked forward to the coming of a new king who would restore Israel to political greatness. Of course, early Christians believed that in some sense Jesus was the king who fulfilled the scriptural prophecies, even though he had not been an earthly monarch.

The title "God's Son" was vague, but suggested someone who shared either in God's divine power or righteousness. In the ancient world, a "son" shared in his father's social status and obediently served him. Hence, "God's Son" naturally suggested anyone who somehow exercised divine authority or who was exemplary in obeying God's law. Not surprisingly, the Hebrew Scriptures call angels "sons of God," since they have superhuman authority from God and serve him perfectly. These Scriptures also occasionally call the nation of Israel (e.g., Exod 4:22) or its king God's "Son" (Ps 2:6–7). By the first century, some Jews were referring to any pious human being as God's son. Thus, Jesus could proclaim that "peacemakers" are "God's sons" (Matt 5:9).

Of course, in the early church, Jesus was supremely God's Son, and every Christian was a child of God by adoption. Thus, Paul could refer to Jesus as God's Son (e.g., Rom 1:3–4) or even as the Son (1 Cor 15:28), and stated that "all who are led by God's Spirit are God's sons" (Rom 8:14).

As Mark proceeds, he will clarify what he means when he writes that Jesus is the "Messiah" and "God's Son." Specifically, he will indicate that Jesus is not a king in this world, but the ruler of the world to come. Jesus exercises the full authority of God and is fully obedient to him.

Questions for Reflection:

Is the story of Jesus' life the good news or only, as Mark suggests, "the beginning of the good news"? In how many different ways is Jesus "God's Son"? In how many ways do Christians become God's sons and daughters through Jesus?

2.   Mark 1:2–8

Just as it is written in Isaiah the prophet, "Look, I am sending out my messenger ahead of you, who will get your road ready"; "a voice of someone crying in the desert, 'Prepare the Lord's road; make his paths straight,'" John the Baptizer appeared in the desert proclaiming a baptism of repentance for forgiveness of sins. And all the countryside of Judea and all the people of Jerusalem went out to him, and they were baptized by him in the Jordan River, as they admitted their sins. Now John was wearing camel's hair and a leather belt around his waist, and he was eating grasshoppers and field honey. And he proclaimed, "A man stronger than I is coming after me. I am not fit to bend down and untie the strap of his sandals. I baptized you by water, but he will baptize you with Holy Spirit" (1:2–8).

The purpose of the opening description of John the Baptist is to point forward to Jesus. Mark shows no interest in John as a figure in his own right. Instead, John's sole aim is to prepare for the coming of Jesus. Indeed, Mark's description assimilates John to the prophet Elijah who was to prepare for the day of the Lord. John's hairy clothes and leather belt remind us of Elijah's appearance as described in 2 Kgs 1:8. "Look, I am sending out my messenger ahead of you, who will get your road ready," alludes to Mal 3:1, and Malachi looks forward to the reappearance of Elijah to prepare Israel for God's coming (4:5–6). The following quotation from Isa 40:3, "Prepare the Lord's road; make his paths straight," reiterates that John's role is only to help people get ready for the coming of a greater one. Strikingly, Mark changes the Isaiah passage slightly. Instead of "God's" paths, Mark uses the word *his* to make it clear that the prophecy points to Jesus. John's subsequent statement that he is not even worthy to untie the sandal strap of this figure and that this "stronger" one will baptize not with water but the Holy Spirit invites the reader to pay special attention to what will occur once this person arrives.

Questions for Reflection:

Is the role of every Christian preacher or teacher to point to Jesus, rather than to oneself? If so, how can we do this?

3.   Mark 1:9–13

And it happened in those days that Jesus came from Nazareth in Galilee and was baptized by John in the Jordan. And at once, as he was coming up out of the water, he saw the heavens torn open and the Spirit coming down as a dove on him. And there was a voice from Heaven, "You are my beloved Son; in you I am delighted" (1:9–11). And at once the Spirit drove him out into the desert, and he was in the desert forty days, tested by Satan, and he was with the wild animals, and the angels waited on him (1:12–13).

Mark links Jesus' baptism and temptation even though they differ utterly. The contrast between these brief scenes could scarcely be greater. The baptism occurs in a river and includes a revelation of God; the temptation occurs in the desert and includes a revelation of Satan. Nevertheless, Mark makes these two scenes a single literary section. The same Holy Spirit which Jesus receives at his baptism "at once" drives him out to be "tested by Satan." Accordingly, in some sense the temptation is the completion of the baptism.

This section gives the reader a fundamental orientation for the entire gospel by suggesting who Jesus is and what his mission will be: Jesus is the Messiah, God's Son, and he must suffer. Thus, on the one hand, the words, "You are my ... Son," recall Psalm 2. There God himself addresses the king of Israel and promises to make the nations obey him. By contrast the words "beloved Son; in you I am delighted" also point to obedient suffering. They allude both to God's order to Abraham to sacrifice his "beloved son" Isaac (Gen 22:2) and to the suffering servant in Isaiah with whom God is pleased (Isa 42:1). Significantly, this information about Jesus, which is so vital for the reader to know, comes from no less an authority than a "voice from heaven."

The scene also hints that Jesus' identity will be a continuing problem in the narrative. As soon as we hear the heavenly voice declare that Jesus is God's beloved Son, we learn that Satan tempts him. Mark gives no explanation concerning what the temptation is. However, the progression suggests that somehow the temptation concerns whether Jesus will be faithful to his vocation as God's "beloved Son." Significantly, Mark does not say the temptation ended once the forty days were over. Later in the gospel various demons will continue to test Jesus by declaring publicly that he is "God's Son" (e.g., 3:11).

The narrative implies that no one but Jesus heard the voice. Even though John baptized Jesus, there is no hint that he was privy to what happened immediately thereafter. On the contrary, the text tells us that it was Jesus who saw the heavens torn open and the Spirit descend on him. The voice addresses him alone. Only much later in the gospel do we have a similar voice from heaven announce to those accompanying Jesus, "This is my beloved Son" (9:7).

The juxtaposition of John's prophecy that the Messiah will baptize with the Holy Spirit and Jesus receiving the Spirit is striking and suggests that Jesus will baptize with the Spirit, but something must happen first. Since Jesus appears immediately

after John's prophecy and receives the Spirit, there can be no
doubt that he is the one who will baptize with the Spirit.
However, the fact that he does not baptize, but instead undergoes temptation from Satan hints that something fundamental
must occur beforehand. The gospel subsequently deals with
what must happen first and ends before narrating the baptism
with the Holy Spirit.

By baptizing with 'the Spirit, Jesus will abolish the barrier
which separates human beings from God. Mark makes this
point by stating that the heavens were "torn open." Within the
biblical tradition, the heavens are a solid dome (a "firma-
ment"), and God dwells above it. Hence, the heavens keep God
and human beings apart. The rending of the heavens and the
coming of the Spirit suggest that there is no separation between
Jesus and God. Hence, when Jesus fulfills John's prophecy by
baptizing with the Holy Spirit, he will enable others to share in
this full access to the divine.

Mark's use of "torn" in this text is odd and invites the
reader to connect this section with the climax of the gospel.
Normally, we do not think of the heavens as something that
could tear. Significantly, both Matthew and Luke "improve"
Mark by stating that the heavens were "opened" (Matt 3:16,
Luke 3:21). As we shall see, at the climax of Mark, the veil of
the temple also is "torn" (15:38). Apart from these two passages
Mark never uses this word, not even when he describes the
action of rending. Instead, Mark tells us that the high priest
"ripped his clothes" (14:63).

Questions for Reflection:

Was it inevitable that, when Jesus was baptized and was
preparing for his public mission, he would experience a new
kind of temptation? Was that testing necessary before he
could baptize others with the Holy Spirit? Why? Is it inevitable that, when Christians today get baptized (or take
some other major step forward in their spiritual lives), we

will experience a new kind of temptation? Will such testing help enable us to be channels of the Holy Spirit for others?

4.　Mark 1:14-20

After John was arrested, Jesus came into Galilee proclaiming God's good news. He said, "The time has come; God's rule has gotten near. Repent and believe the good news" (1:14–15).

And as he was passing by, along the Sea of Galilee, he saw Simon and Andrew, Simon's brother, casting in the sea, for they were fishermen. And Jesus said to them, "Follow me, and I will make you become fishers for human beings." And at once, leaving the nets, they followed him. And going on a little, he saw James, Zebedee's son, and John his brother who were in the boat repairing the nets. And at once he called them, and leaving their father, Zebedee, in the boat with the hired hands, they went away after him (1:16–20).

These verses clearly indicate that a new section of the narrative is beginning. John the Baptist, who dominated the opening section of the gospel, now passes from the scene. Jesus then announces "the time has come," and he begins to summon his followers.

Yet, even as Mark indicates that a new phase of the story is beginning, he carefully suggests that we are still in a period of preparation. Jesus tells Simon and Andrew not that he is now making them "fishers for human beings," but only that one day he will.

In this section, we get the first of many indications that Mark is writing primarily for Christians. In these verses Mark writes as if the persons and events to which he refers are familiar and so require no explanation. Thus, he does not tell us why John was arrested or who Simon is. He assumes we know. Presumably, the only audience which would necessarily have such knowledge would be members of the church. For such readers, John's arrest would point forward to the death of Jesus.

To these readers, the scene is a reminder that we must follow Jesus without hesitation, no matter what the cost. As the first disciples whom Jesus calls, Simon (Peter), Andrew, James, and John symbolize anyone who would be a disciple. Strikingly, the text emphasizes that Jesus takes the initiative by summoning them. Peter and Andrew then follow Jesus at once, and James and John abandon everything, even their father, and follow. Later we will see that following Jesus without hesitation, no matter what the cost, is a central theme in Mark and addresses a specific crisis in his Christian community.

Questions for Reflection:

How long do we have to follow Jesus before we can proclaim him? What strengths and weaknesses do new followers of Jesus often have?

5.   Mark 1:21–39

And they entered Capernaum, and at once on the Sabbath he went into the synagogue and taught. And they were astonished at his teaching, for he was teaching them like someone who has authority and not as the scribes. And at once there was in their synagogue a person with an unclean spirit, and he shouted out, "What do you have to do with us, Jesus of Nazareth? You have come to ruin us!

*I know you, who you are, God's Holy One!" And Jesus repri-
manded him, "Shut up and come out of him!" And after the
unclean spirit convulsed him and cried out in a loud voice, he
came out of him. And all were amazed and so discussed with each
other, "What is this? A new teaching with authority! He gives orders
even to the unclean spirits, and they listen to him!" And a rumor
about him at once went out everywhere into the whole surrounding
region of Galilee (1:21–28).*

*And at once they came out of the synagogue and came into the
house of Simon and Andrew, with James and John. Now Simon's
mother-in-law was lying down feverish, and at once they spoke to
him about her. And he came to her and grasped her hand and got
her up, and the fever left her, and she waited on them (1:29–31).*

*And when it became evening, when the sun had set, they kept
bringing to him all who were sick and possessed with demons. And
the entire city was gathered by the door, and he healed many who
were sick with various illnesses, and he drove out many demons,
and he would not let the demons speak, because they knew him
(1:32–34).*

*And early, while it was still very dark, he arose and came out and
went away into a deserted place, and there he began to pray. And
Simon and those who were with him hunted him, and they found
him and said to him, "All are seeking you." And he said to them,
"Let's go elsewhere to the neighboring towns, so I may preach there
also, for I came out for this." And he went preaching in their
synagogues in the whole of Galilee and driving out demons
(1:35–39).*

This section makes it clear for the first time that the temptation Jesus faces is to gain public approval by becoming
known as God's Son. As we saw above, earlier in the gospel just
after God declares that Jesus is his Son, Satan tempts him.
However, the gospel does not specify what the temptation is. In
this section, we now learn that the demons (who presumably
are in league with Satan) repeatedly try to publicize the fact that
Jesus is God's Son. Jesus silences them. Thus, in the story of the

person with the unclean spirit, the demon shouts publicly that Jesus is "God's Holy One," and Jesus must silence it. Similarly, in a summary of many miracles, Mark states, "He would not let the demons speak, because they knew him." Of course, proclaiming that Jesus is God's Son makes the public lionize him. Indeed, Mark emphasizes that the first miracle makes Jesus famous throughout the region.

To avoid public approval, Jesus works his miracles only in private or withdraws quickly as soon as he works them in public. He performs his first miracle only after the demon confronts him, and as soon as he performs the exorcism and so provokes public admiration, Jesus retires into Simon's house. There in private, he heals Simon's mother-in-law. Then when the whole town besieges him, he does heal many people. However, once again as soon as possible he withdraws to a deserted location. When Simon and his companions succeed in tracking him down and make him aware that everyone is looking for him, he insists on going away to neighboring towns. Subsequently, he performs exorcisms throughout Galilee, but keeps on the move.

Strikingly, Mark emphasizes that Jesus' mission is primarily to teach and preach rather than to work miracles. At the beginning of the story about the person with the unclean spirit, Mark stresses that Jesus is teaching with authority. Indeed, people are astonished. The exorcism is practically an interruption. The demon noisily confronts Jesus, and he must take action. Even the exorcism itself can be described as "a new teaching." Later, when Simon and the others track Jesus down and Jesus insists on going elsewhere, he declares he must preach, for that is why he began his work.

Questions for Reflection:

> Can popularity be a danger for the Christian missionary? Why? In general, is preaching more important than miracle working? Can a true miracle be a kind of teaching?

⇥ ✳ ⇤

6.   Mark 1:40-45

*And a leper came to him and, begging him, knelt down and said
to him, "If you want, you can make me clean." And becoming
angry, he stretched out his hand and touched him and said to him,
"I do want; be clean." And at once the leprosy left him, and he was
made clean. And after he snarled at him, he at once threw him out
and said to him, "See that you say nothing to anyone, but go off,
show yourself to the priest and offer for your cleansing what Moses
commanded, as proof for them." But he went out and began to
proclaim it a great deal and to spread the word, so he could no
longer come into a city openly, but was out in deserted places, yet
they kept coming to him from everywhere (1:40-45).*

In response to the unwanted popularity Jesus increases his
efforts to avoid public acclaim. Jesus tries so hard that his
actions become disturbing. The leper acts with extreme defer-
ence. His request leaves open the possibility that Jesus may not
want to heal him. Yet Jesus responds harshly. As soon as the
healing occurs, Jesus "snarls" and throws the man out, warning
him not to talk to anyone. In all probability, Jesus' response is
even harsher than we have noted so far. According to some
ancient manuscripts, the leper actually knelt before Jesus when
making his request, and other manuscripts record that Jesus
became angry at the man. Since it is much easier to see why
ancient copyists may have omitted such features rather than
adding them, I am inclined to think they come from Mark
himself. Mark included them to stress how reluctant Jesus is to
work a miracle which might lead to public enthusiasm.

As part of this increasing effort to avoid popular acclaim,
Jesus now demands that a miracle be kept secret. Previously,
Jesus openly worked miracles and tried only to prevent the

demons from revealing his identity. Now for the first time, he attempts to suppress the knowledge that he has healed some- one and, therefore, orders the man to "say nothing to anyone."

Nevertheless, Jesus' efforts fail, and once again he must withdraw. The man disobeys the order and publicizes the mir- acle. Consequently, Jesus retreats into the uninhabited coun- tryside.

By disobeying Jesus' urgent command, the man shows a profound lack of faith. At the beginning of the story, the man expresses at least some confidence in Jesus by saying, "You can make me clean." Once Jesus cleanses him, however, the man breaks faith. Jesus' order is emphatic, "See that you say nothing to anyone." Yet, the man violates it utterly. He proclaims the news "a great deal" and spreads the word. Later, Mark will emphasize that faith primarily consists of persistently seeking and following Jesus.

Questions for Reflection:

Should some miracles be kept quiet? Do miracles some- times generate the wrong kind of publicity and confuse people about what Christianity actually is?

7.   Mark 2:1–12

And when he came back into Capernaum after some days, it was learned that he was at home. And many gathered so there was no longer room, not even in the area by the door, and he was speaking the word to them. And some came bringing to him a paralyzed man who was being carried by four people. And when they could not bring the man to him because of the crowd, they removed the roof where he was, and when they had dug through, they let down the cot where the paralyzed man was lying. And when Jesus saw their faith, he said to the paralyzed man, "Child, your sins are forgiven." Now some of the scribes were sitting there and thinking in their hearts, "Why does this fellow talk this way? He is committing blasphemy! Who can forgive sins, except the one God?" And at once Jesus perceived in his spirit that they were thinking this way in themselves, and he said to them, "Why are you thinking these things in your hearts? What is easier: to say to the paralyzed man, 'Your sins are forgiven' or to say, 'Get up, and pick up your cot and walk'? But so you know that the son of humanity has authority on earth to forgive sins." He said to the paralyzed man, "I say to you, get up, pick up your cot, and go off to your house." And he got up, and at once, picking up the cot, he went out before everyone, so all were beside themselves and glorified God, saying, "We never saw something like this!" (2:1–12).

Within the overall structure of Mark's gospel, this story makes a bridge between two sections. The story of the healing of the paralytic, climaxes the series of miracles which begins with the exorcism in 1:21–28. At the same time, the controversy between Jesus and the scribes introduces a series of confrontations between Jesus and his detractors. This series climaxes in 3:1–6 when Jesus performs a healing on the Sabbath and, as a result, the Pharisees and Herodians decide to kill him.

Mark probably combined two narratives to produce 2:1–12. When people told and retold stories about Jesus, it seems likely they would have simplified and so not recounted an argument between Jesus and his critics within a larger miracle narrative. Be that as it may, it is striking that the controversy between Jesus and his critics over who can forgive sins (2:5b–10a) fits awkwardly into the larger story. Indeed, the section ends with an incomplete sentence ("But so you know that the son of humanity has authority on earth to forgive sins"). Interestingly, Mark brackets the section with the same words, "He said to the paralyzed man." It also seems very probable that Mark inserted a story in which Jesus claimed to be able to forgive sins within a story of Jesus healing a paralyzed man. To make the insertion, Mark introduced the controversy after the words, "He said to the paralyzed man," and then repeated these same words when he resumed the description of the miracle.

The story of the healing of the paralyzed man emphasizes that Jesus deliberately works the miracle in public. The narrative stresses that an enormous number of witnesses are present. Indeed, the crowd is so great that there is no room even by the door, and the four men who are carrying the paralytic are reduced to digging through the roof and lowering the man down the hole. Moreover, the story underlines the fact that the miracle is worked in plain view of all, "Picking up the cot, he went out before everyone." Indeed, the purpose of the miracle is, at least in part, to give a visible demonstration to Jesus' critics that he has the power to forgive sins.

Coming right after the cleansing of the leper, the public character of the healing is striking. In the earlier story, Jesus orders the leper to "say nothing to anyone." Now immediately afterward, Jesus himself performs a public healing.

In this second story, Jesus' action primarily provokes rejection rather than popularity. Thanks to Mark's editing, Jesus works the miracle in response to objections from his critics. To be sure, everyone then glorifies God. However, within the larger context, this is the first of a series of confrontations between Jesus and his opponents which only a chapter later provokes them to decide to kill him.

In the story, Jesus works the public miracle in response to exemplary faith, and this faith is shown by persistence in coming to Jesus. The story stresses the difficulty which the four people who are seeking the miracle have in reaching him. They are not able to get through the crowd. Consequently, they take the extreme step of lugging the paralytic up onto the roof, digging through it and lowering the cot down the hole. The persistence shows their trust in Jesus, and the story stresses that it is this faith that leads Jesus to act. It was "when Jesus saw their faith" that he turned his attention to helping the man.

The story also suggests that Jesus will willingly work a public miracle if only it either provokes public rejection or else bears public witness to someone's faith.

This story introduces the title "son of humanity" which subsequently will be important in the narrative. Jesus declares that, as the son of humanity, he has authority to forgive sins. Later in the gospel, as we shall see, Mark uses this title to balance the designation "Messiah." Jesus is both the Messiah and the "son of humanity."

For Mark and his readers, the title, son of humanity, suggested that Jesus was a human being and also that he was the one through whom God would judge and rule the world. In both Hebrew and Aramaic the phrase "son of humanity" is a synonym for "human being." Even though Mark wrote in Greek, it is clear that he and his readers were aware of this meaning. In 3:28, Jesus declares, "All sins and blasphemies will be forgiven to the sons of human beings." Here, the term in the plural can only mean "people." The title "son of humanity," also appears in Dan 7:13–14 and refers to a superhuman figure at the final judgment who receives dominion over the world. Later, Mark's gospel will apply this title to Jesus as the one who will return in glory to judge the world and then reign over it (8:38, 13:26–27).

Because Jesus is both a human being and the final judge of the world, he has authority to forgive sins on earth. Since he is human, he experiences the sufferings and temptations that people face and so is in a position to set standards. As the final judge, he will ultimately be the one who will declare who is innocent and who is guilty. This gives him the right, even now, to pronounce forgiveness by God's authority. His critics are correct when they object, "Who can forgive sins, except the one God?" What they do not realize is that Jesus is God's Son and rightly exercises God's prerogatives.

Questions for Reflection:

Would God be in a position to judge us if he never faced the sufferings and temptations we do? Do Christians today have the authority to pronounce forgiveness in God's name? Will we heal people if we pronounce forgiveness? To exercise this authority properly, do we need to experience the sufferings of the sinner and his or her victims?If we exercise this authority, will we often experience rejection?

8.   Mark 2:13-28

And he went back out beside the sea. And all the crowd came to him, and he taught them. And as he was passing by, he saw Levi, the son of Alphaeus, sitting at the tax office, and he said to him, "Follow me." And he rose and followed him. And he dined in his house, and many tax collectors and sinners were eating with Jesus and his students, for there were many, and they were following him. And when the scribes of the Pharisees saw that he was eating with the sinners and tax collectors, they kept saying to his students, "He eats with the tax collectors and sinners!" And when Jesus heard this, he said to them, "Those who are healthy have no need of a doctor, but those who are sick; I did not come to call the righteous, but sinners" (2:13–17).

And John's students and the Pharisees were fasting. And they came and said to him, "For what reason do John's students and the students of the Pharisees fast, but your students do not fast?" And Jesus said to them, "The groom's party cannot fast while the groom is with them, can they? For as long as they have the groom with them, they cannot fast. But the days will come when the groom will be taken away from them, and then they will fast on that day. No one sews a patch from a piece of unshrunken cloth on an old garment. Otherwise, the fullness of the new will pull away from the old, and there will be a worse tear. And no one puts new wine into old wineskins. Otherwise, the wine will burst the skins, and the wine is lost and so are the skins. But new wine is put into new skins" (2:18–22).

And while he was passing by through the grain fields on the Sabbath, his students began to make their way by picking the heads of grain. And the Pharisees said to him, "See what they are doing on the Sabbath! It is not allowed!" And he said to them, "Have you never read what David did when he was in need and he himself was hungry along with those who were with him, how he went into God's house during the high priesthood of Abiathar and ate the bread of presentation which it is not allowed for anyone except the priests to eat, and he gave it also to those who were with him?" And he said to them, "The Sabbath was made for humanity, not humanity for the Sabbath. So then, the son of humanity is Lord even of the Sabbath" (2:23–2:28).

Much of the specific material here was relatively unimportant to Mark and his intended readers. The issue of whether it was allowable to pick grain on the Sabbath probably did not concern Mark's Gentile audience. Similarly, the attack on followers of Jesus for not fasting was no longer even accurate. As the story itself makes clear, once Jesus was dead, the early church did fast.

For the gospel as a whole, these stories are significant because they suggest that relations between Jesus and his critics are deteriorating. In each of these stories, there is a confrontation between Jesus and his faultfinders. Accordingly, the theme of opposition which we first encounter in the story of the healing of the paralytic intensifies. Mark makes the threat more menacing by attributing it to a continuing source, namely the Pharisees. Some of the references to the Pharisees in these stories are problematic. The two phrases "the scribes of the Pharisees" and "the students of the Pharisees" are awkward and unclear. In the sources Mark used, the criticism of Jesus' association with sinners probably came simply from the scribes, and the criticism of not fasting came simply from John's students. Mark added references to the Pharisees in order to emphasize a growing threat. In keeping with the growing menace, Mark gives us the first clear intimation of Jesus' approaching death. Jesus is the bridegroom, and "the days will come when the groom will be taken away."

Once again, we encounter the theme that Jesus is the son of humanity and, therefore, has authority over sin. Because as "the son of humanity" he is a human being and the final judge of the world, he is also Lord of the Sabbath. Hence, he can excuse his followers from the need to obey the Sabbath regulations.

It appears that Mark added this concluding comment about the son of humanity's authority to the story of picking grain on the Sabbath. The previous sentence, "The Sabbath was made for humanity, not humanity for the Sabbath" would provide an admirable conclusion to the narrative. By contrast, the following comment about the son of humanity does not follow logically and so seems out of place. Perhaps then, Mark himself added it to a preexisting story.

Questions for Reflection:

Does much of the Bible deal with issues which at least superficially are no longer relevant? Do such portions of Scripture still contain a deeper message that remains significant? If so, how can we find that message? What did Jesus say to his own time when he ate with social outcasts? What does he say to us?

9.   Mark 3:1–6

And again he went into the synagogue, and a person was there who had a paralyzed hand. And they were watching him carefully to see if he would heal him on the Sabbath, so they could bring charges against him. And he said to the person who had the paralyzed hand, "Stand up, and go to the center." And he said to them, "Is it allowable on the Sabbath to do good or to do evil, to save life or to kill?" But they were silent. And after he looked around at them with anger, grieved over their hardheadedness, he said to the person, "Hold out your hand." And he held it out, and his hand was restored. And at once the Pharisees went out and plotted against him with the Herodians in order to destroy him (3:1–6).

With this story Mark brings the series of conflicts between Jesus and his religious critics to a climax. At the end of this confrontation Jesus' critics withdraw and start plotting to kill him.

This story has striking similarities to the one in 2:1–11 which begins the series. In both 2:1–11 and here, Jesus spars with religious lawyers over his own authority. In the first story, the issue is whether Jesus has the right to forgive sins. Here it is whether he may heal on the Sabbath. In both stories, Jesus asks a confrontational question. In the first, the question is whether it is easier to say someone's sins are forgiven or to heal. In the second, the question is whether it is permissible to do good on the Sabbath. Then, in both accounts, he heals a paralyzed man.

This last story in the series reinforces the point that the first story makes: Jesus is willing to work public miracles as long as they incite rejection. Here, Jesus deliberately works a miracle before his enemies. However, the miracle is the culmination of an increasingly bitter confrontation and sets in motion a plot against him. Thus, at the opening of the story, Jesus' enemies are waiting to see if he will work a miracle "so they could bring

charges against him." Jesus shows that he knows their agenda
by raising the question of whether what he is doing is legal.
When they are silent, he looks at them with disappointment and
anger. Consequently, the following miracle is a deliberate pro-
vocation and, not surpisingly, results in a conspiracy to do away
with him.

Questions for Reflection:

Can religious people often be narrow and "hardheaded"?
What leads to such lack of compassion and flexibility? Will
a Christian who challenges these attitudes normally experience rejection, even if he or she does great things in Jesus'
name?

10.   Mark 3:7-12

*And Jesus with his disciples withdrew toward the sea, and a great
throng from Galilee and Judea and from Jerusalem and from
Idumea and across the Jordan and from around Tyre and Sidon
followed, a great throng, since they were hearing how much he was
doing. They came to him, and he spoke to his students so that a
boat might stand ready for him on account of the crowd so they
would not crush him (for he healed many, so that all who had
afflictions would fall on him in order to touch him). And the
unclean spirits, whenever they saw him, were falling down before
him and would shout, "You are God's Son." And he reprimanded
them a lot so they would not make him known (3:7-12).*

This long summary concludes a major section of the gospel
(1:14-3:12) by reemphasizing that Jesus withdraws after
working public miracles and tries to hide his identity as God's
Son to avoid public acclaim. Near the beginning of the section,

Jesus muzzles unclean spirits who proclaim publicly that he is "God's Holy One," and withdraws as soon as he works wonders that would make him popular (1:21–29). Then, he insists publicly that he is a human being ("son of humanity") and deliberately incites opposition. Here, at the end of the section he again works miracles with reluctance. Immediately after he heals the withered hand, he withdraws toward the sea, but cannot escape the crowds. They have heard "how much he was doing" and demand healing. As Jesus confronts the evil spirits, they try to expose his identity, and he must silence them. Significantly, Mark ends the section, not with an account of a single healing, but with a summary of numerous ones. He suggests that in this part of the gospel Jesus' constant concern is to keep his true identity hidden to avoid fanning public enthusiasm.

This summary also helps prepare for the next major section when Jesus begins to reveal to his intimate students who he is and starts to teach them (and the reader) that he and his followers must patiently endure.

Questions for Reflection:

Can someone proclaim publicly that Jesus is God's Son and yet use that proclamation to mislead people about what the Christian message is? Should we sometimes ask such people to stop their preaching?

11.   Mark 3:13–19

And he went up on the mountain, and he summoned those whom he wanted, and they went away to him. And he appointed twelve that they might be with him and that he might send them out to preach and to have authority to drive out demons: Peter (the name he also gave to Simon) and James, the son of Zebedee, and John, James's brother (and to them he gave the names "Boanerges," that is "Sons of Thunder") and Andrew and Philip and Bartholomew and Matthew and Thomas and James, Alphaeus's son, and Thaddaeus and Simon the Zealous and Judas Iscariot, who also betrayed him (3:13–19).

Mark begins a new section of the gospel by emphasizing that Jesus chooses some people to be his intimate students, and this choice separates them from the world. Jesus withdraws by going up on a mountain. Then he summons twelve, and they go away to him. Their role now is to be with him and to share his authority and ministry.

Mark's original Christian readers would have tended to identify with the disciples, especially with Peter. The disciples answer Jesus' summons and share in his ministry. Peter is the first disciple Jesus calls in Mark's gospel and the first in the list of the twelve. To some degree, each of Mark's intended Christian readers also had answered a summons from Jesus and at least aspired to share in his ministry. Accordingly, they would have assumed that what happens to the disciples in general and Peter in particular was especially relevant.

Consequently, the mistakes that these disciples make in the subsequent narrative would have served as warnings to the original readers to do better.

Questions for Reflection:

In what ways does following Jesus separate us from the world? How are Christians today like the twelve apostles in Mark's gospel? How are we different? Can we identify with them?

12.   Mark 3:20-35

And he went into a house, and again a crowd assembled so that they could not even eat food. And when his relatives heard, they came out to seize him, for they were saying, "He is beside himself." And the scribes who had come down from Jerusalem were saying, "He is in the grasp of Beelzebul," and, "By the ruler of the demons he drives out demons." And when he had summoned them, he spoke to them using comparisons: "How can Satan drive out Satan? And if a kingdom is divided against itself, that kingdom cannot stand. And if a house is divided against itself, that house will not be able to stand. And if Satan has risen against himself and is divided, he cannot stand but is at an end. Indeed, no one can enter into a strong man's house to loot his stuff unless they first tie up the strong man, and then they will loot his house. Truly, I say to you that all sins and blasphemies will be forgiven to the sons of human beings, no matter how much they blaspheme. But whoever blasphemes against the Holy Spirit does not ever have forgiveness, but is guilty of an eternal sin," because they were saying, "He has an unclean spirit" (3:20–30).

And his mother and his brothers and sisters came, and standing outside, they sent word to him that they were summoning him. Now a crowd was sitting around him, and they said to him, "Look, your mother and your brothers and your sisters are asking for you outside." And in reply he said to them, "Who are my mother and brothers and sisters?" And looking around at those who were sitting about him in a circle, he said, "Here are my mother and my brothers and sisters; whoever does God's will, this is my brother and sister and mother!" (3:31–35).

In this section, Mark has placed together a number of stories and sayings which were originally separate . We begin with the disturbing—and, therefore, surely historical—narrative that Jesus' family thought he was out of his mind and tried to seize him. Next, we have a charge from Jesus' critics that he drives out demons by Beelzebul. To this, Jesus gives two different replies: First, Satan would not cast out Satan. Second, Jesus can only cast out Satan after tieing him up. Then Mark includes the saying about the sin against the Spirit. In other early Christian literature this saying occurs separately (Luke 12:10; Gospel of Thomas 44). To place this saying within the story, Mark adds the words, "because they were saying, 'He has an unclean spirit.'" Finally, we have the story that when Jesus' family seeks him, Jesus says that his real family is those who do God's will.

The theme of the section Mark has produced by combining this material is that Jesus' disciples replace his natural family. This section discredits Jesus' natural mother and siblings. At the beginning of the passage, they assume he is crazy and set out to seize him, and at the end when they actually arrive, Jesus declines to speak with them. Mark stresses that Jesus' natural family remains "outside." Indeed, by sandwiching the other material between these glimpses of Jesus' family, Mark implies that Jesus' mother and siblings are scarcely better than the scribes who charge that Jesus is in league with Satan. By contrast, at the climax of the section, Mark notes that the disciples are "sitting about" Jesus, and Jesus insists that his students who do God's will are his true "brother and sister and mother." Of course, Mark's readers can choose to be part of this family.

Questions for Reflection:

Does faithfulness to Jesus sometimes make people act in ways that others consider to be insanity? What does it mean to be part of Jesus' family?

13.   Mark 4:1–25

And again he began to teach beside the sea, and a very great crowd gathered by him so he got into a boat and sat on the sea, and all the crowd were on the land beside the sea. And he taught them many things in parables. He said to them in his teaching, "Listen! Look, a sower went out to sow. And during the sowing, it happened that some seed fell beside the road, and the birds came and ate it up. And other seed fell on the rocky ground where it did not have much earth, and, at once, it sprouted up because it had no deep earth. And when the sun rose, it was scorched, and because it had no root, it withered. And other seed fell in the thorns, and the thorns came up and choked it, and it did not produce fruit. And other seeds fell on the good earth, and coming up and growing, it kept producing fruit. One seed bore thirtyfold and another sixty and another a hundred." And he said, "Whoever has ears to hear, hear" (4:1–9).

And when he was alone, those who were around him together with the twelve asked him about the parables. And he said to them, "To you the mystery of God's rule has been given, but to those outside everything is in parables, so they may look and look, and not see, and listen and listen, and not understand, lest they convert and receive forgiveness" (4:10–12).

And he said to them, "Do you not understand this parable? And how will you comprehend all the parables? 'The sower' sows the word. And these are the ones 'beside the road' where the word is sown. When they hear it, at once Satan comes and removes the word which was sown in them. And similarly these are the ones sown 'on the rocky ground.' When they hear the word, at once they receive it with joy. Yet they do not have a root in themselves but are temporary. Then when oppression or persecution occurs because of the word, at once they fall away. And the others sown 'in the thorns,' these are they who hear the word, and the worries of this world and the lure of wealth and desires for the other things penetrate them and choke the word, and it becomes fruitless. And those which were sown on 'the good earth' are whoever hear the word and accept it and bear fruit, one thirtyfold and one sixty and one a hundred" (4:13–20).

And he said to them, "A lamp is not brought in to be put under a bucket or under a bed, is it? Rather to be put on a stand! For there is nothing hidden except to be made known, and nothing is hidden away, but so it may come to be known. If anyone has ears to hear, hear" (4:21–23).

And he said to them, "Pay attention to what you hear. By the measure which you measure, it will be measured out to you. And more will be added for you. For whoever has, it will be given to them, and whoever does not have, even what they do have will be taken away from them" (4:24–25).

In this section, Mark passes on several different sayings which go back to Jesus and one which probably came from early Christian preaching. The Parable of the Sower, the exhortation to hear, and the following sayings about a lamp, about what is hidden being revealed, about receiving back the measure we give, and about those who have gained more, almost certainly come from Jesus. By contrast, the words about looking and not seeing are based on Isa 6:9–10, and it was probably early Christians who first used them to explain why many outsiders rejected the Christian message. The Gospel of John also resorts to Isa 6:10 to explain why people did not believe in Jesus, and in John the quotation does not appear in Jesus' own words, but in a comment from the evangelist (John 12:39–40).

It may well be, however, that Mark himself composed the interpretation of the Parable of the Sower. In the apocryphal *Gospel of Thomas* (log. 9), the Parable of the Sower appears without an appended explanation. Historically, it seems likely that Jesus used parables to help his audiences understand his message, rather than make it totally obscure. Surely, if Jesus did not want the crowds to understand and repent, he would not have bothered to preach to them. Moreover, the explanation of the parable seems less suited to the time of Jesus than to that of the early church. It was in the later era that such things as persecution arose.

For Mark, the Parable of the Sower with its appended explanation contains the key to Jesus' message. Earlier, the gospel mentions that Jesus was teaching with authority (1:21–27), but we receive no information as to what that teaching was. Now, with the Parable of the Sower and its explanation, we have the first extended presentation of Jesus' message. Before giving the explanation, Jesus says that if his students do not understand this parable, they will not understand any parable. Mark is now providing us with the essence of what Jesus has to tell us.

The point of the parable with its appended explanation is that people who hear Jesus' words must endure with patience in order to bear fruit. In the first half of the parable and its explanation, we have a series of groups who hear the word but do not endure. Some forget the word almost immediately; others fall away because of persecution; still others forsake the gospel to pursue worldly success. None of these bear fruit. The second half of the parable and its explanation tell us that there are other people who do go on to bear fruit abundantly.

Mark suggests that this message must be preached to the world at a later time, as it cannot be preached yet. Indeed, Jesus talks in parables so that no one but his students will understand. Nevertheless, as soon as Jesus privately explains what the parable means, he insists there is nothing hidden which will not be revealed. The gospel is a lamp, and no one brings in a lamp only to hide it. Mark emphasizes this point by adding the words, "If anyone has ears to hear, let him hear." Accordingly, the time to share the message hidden in the parable will surely come. Later in Mark's gospel, Jesus will insist that "the good news must . . . be proclaimed to all the nations" (13:10).

Mark's Greek suggests that Jesus is the lamp which will be hidden temporarily and then give light to all. The Greek in 4:21–22 is ambiguous—apparently deliberately so. One could also translate it, "A lamp does not come to be put under a bucket or under a bed, does it? Rather to be put on a stand! For it is not hidden except to be made known; and it was not hidden away, but so it may come to be known." Of course, in Mark's gospel Jesus is the one who "comes" (e.g., 1:14), and elsewhere in the New Testament he is explicitly called a "lamp" (Rev 21:23).

The reason the message of Jesus cannot yet be preached is that prior to the crucifixion outsiders have no hope of understanding the need for patient endurance. The parable itself suggests that even after Jesus has given the supreme example of patient endurance, most people who hear the word will still fall away because of such things as persecution or the lure of wealth. Accordingly, Jesus would not be doing outsiders a favor by preaching his message clearly before his death. The crowds might indeed turn and be forgiven. However, they would later desert and so end up worse off than if they had never really heard the good news.

Indeed, as we shall see, even the students to whom Jesus explains the need for patient endurance will fall away prior to the crucifixion, and this section of Mark begins to prepare us for the disaster. When Jesus tells the parable, the disciples do not understand it. After Jesus explains it, he warns them to beware as they listen. Those who fail to understand will lose even what they have. Subsequently, as we shall see, the disciples do lose everything. Here in chapter 4, Jesus says that it is outsiders who look and do not see and listen and do not understand. However, a few chapters later after his students have remained obtuse, Jesus will tell them that they have eyes and yet do not see and ears and do not hear (8:18).

Of course, Mark's intended Christian readers lived in the era when endurance could be proclaimed and had to be lived. Jesus had already been crucified, and so they had to be steadfast both in preaching and practicing the truth.

Questions for Reflection:

Do most people in our time who initially become enthusiastic about religion later fall away? Do they do so for the same reasons Jesus gives in the explanation of the Parable of the Sower or for other reasons? What would patient endurance in being a Christian involve in our own situations today?

14.   Mark 4:26-34

And he said, "God's rule is like this: It is as if a person throws seed on the earth. And he sleeps and rises, night and day, and the seed sprouts and becomes long. How, he does not know. On its own the earth bears fruit, first the blade, then the ear, then the full grain in the ear, but whenever the fruit is ripe, at once he puts in the sickle because the harvest stands ready" (4:26–29).

And he said, "How shall we compare God's rule or with what parable shall we put it? It is like a mustard seed, which when it is sown on earth is the smallest of all the seeds on earth. Yet when it is sown, it comes up and becomes bigger than all vegetables and produces big branches so the birds of the sky can nest under its shadow" (4:30–32).

And with many such parables he kept speaking the word to them as they were able to hear it, but without a parable he did not speak to them, but in private to his own students he kept explaining everything (4:33–34).

After using the Parable of the Sower to emphasize the need for patient endurance, Mark passes on two other parables which further this message. Both the Parable of the Seed Growing by Itself and the Parable of the Mustard Seed emphasize the contrast between the small beginnings of God's rule and its ultimate greatness. Hence, in the larger context Mark provides, they reinforce the teaching that Jesus' followers must wait patiently.

Mark ends the section on parables by stressing that Jesus spells out his message to his students but not to outsiders.

Once more, Mark hints that later it will be time to share the full message with the multitudes. Both the Parable of the Seed Growing by Itself and the Parable of the Mustard Seed suggest that the kingdom which is now small will grow to include vast numbers of people. Mark tells us that Jesus spoke to the crowd "as they were able to hear." As of yet, they could not fully hear. However, when God's rule expands, they too will be able to understand.

Questions for Reflection:

Is the way that God's power enters our lives (whether as individuals or as communities) fundamentally mysterious? Is it sometimes a mistake to try to explain everything, especially to people who are spiritually immature?

15.   Mark 4:35–41

That day, when it became evening, he said to them, "Let's go over to the other side." And leaving the crowd, they took him along as he was in the boat, and other boats were with him. And a strong windstorm came up, and the waves splashed into the boat so the boat was already starting to be filled. Yet, he was in the stern, sleeping on the cushion. And they roused him and said to him, "Teacher, do you not care that we are dying?" And when he was fully awake, he reprimanded the wind and said to the sea, "Settle down; shut up!" And the wind stopped, and there was a great calm. And he said to them, "Why are you scared? Don't you have faith yet?" And they became greatly afraid and said to each other, "Then who is this that even the wind and the sea listen to him?" (4:35–41).

After Jesus has taught the disciples verbally about the need for patient endurance, he begins to teach them—and the reader—the same lesson through his deeds. He invites his students to cross the lake. A storm arises. Yet he remains asleep. Finally, when the boat is about to sink, they become desperate and wake him up. He saves them, and then reprimands them for cowardice. If they had only trusted him more, they would have endured the storm longer.

The story suggests that the reason Jesus' followers should be able to endure is that he exercises the very power of God himself. In the Hebrew Scriptures, only God can control the elements (e.g., Ps 107:23–30). Here, Jesus controls the wind and the sea. Hence, his students need not fear. Significantly, the story dramatically concludes with the disciples wondering who Jesus might be.

As we shall see, the stilling of the storm is only the first in a series of miracles in which Jesus challenges his students to endure and hints to them who he is.

This opening story suggests that the disciples will fail to meet the challenge because they do not pay enough attention to Jesus. In the story the disciples fail completely. They do not endure the storm, and Jesus must reprimand them for cowardice. They also do not perceive who Jesus is and so the story ends with them wondering who he could be. Perhaps it is Mark's need to foreshadow the reason for their failure which explains the odd details near the beginning of the narrative. Thus, it is strange that Mark tells us the disciples took Jesus along "as he was in the boat," and it is even stranger that he mentions "and other boats were with him." Subsequently, these play no role in the story, and since the disciples have already left the crowd, it is not even clear whose boats these could be. I would suggest that Mark added the odd details to hint that the disciples are not paying attention to Jesus. Even though he was the one who proposed that they go across the lake, they took him along mostly by accident. Since he was already in the boat, they let him stay even though he could have used another vessel.

Questions for Reflection:

What is faith? Must genuine faith include a willingness to persist in following Jesus despite obstacles and danger? Does it sometimes seem in times of crisis that God does not care? What can we do to perceive more clearly at times of crisis who Jesus is and that he does care?

16.   Mark 5:1-20

And they came to the other side of the sea to the district of the Gerasenes. And when he had come out of the boat, at once a person from the tombs who had an unclean spirit met him. He had his dwelling in the tombs, and no one was able any longer to bind him, not even with a chain (because often he had been bound with fetters and shackles, and the shackles were pulled apart by him, and the fetters were shattered), and no one was strong enough to subdue him. And all night and day in the tombs and on the mountains he was shouting and cutting himself up with stones. And when he saw Jesus from a distance, he ran and knelt down before him. And shouting in a loud voice he said, "What have we got to do with each other, Jesus, Son of God Most High? I implore you in God's name, do not torture me!" (for Jesus was saying to him, "Unclean spirit, come out of the person"). And he asked him, "What is your name?" And he said to him, "'Legion' is my name because we are many." And he begged him much that he would not send them out of the district (5:1–10).

Now, there toward the hill a big herd of pigs was grazing. And they begged him, "Send us into the pigs that we may enter them." And he gave them permission. And the unclean spirits came out and entered into the pigs, and the herd, numbering about two thousand, rushed down the slope into the sea and drowned in the sea. And the people who were tending them fled and spread the news in the city and in the countryside, and people came to see what it was that had happened. And they came to Jesus and saw the man who had been possessed seated, clothed, and sane, the one who had the legion, and they became afraid. And the people who had seen told them what happened to the man who was possessed and about the pigs. And they began to beg him to go away from their territory. And as he was getting into the boat, the man who had been possessed begged him that he might be with him. Yet he did not let him but said to him, "Go off to your home and to your relatives and tell them how much the Lord has done for you and had mercy on you." And he went away and began to proclaim in the Decapolis how much Jesus had done for him, and all marvelled (5:11–20).

Healing stories, especially when passed on orally, tended to follow a set outline in the era when Mark was writing. First, there was a description of the problem. Often this description emphasized the gravity of someone's condition. Then, there would be an account of the specific actions that the miracle worker took to effect the cure. Finally, we would have a visible sign that the miracle had taken place. Often the recounting of this sign stressed the dramatic suddenness and certainty of the cure and the amazement of the onlookers.

On the whole, Mark's description of the healing of the man with the legion follows the typical outline well, and we can assume that Mark faithfully passed on the story he heard. Mark presents the man's desperate condition in moving detail. He then recounts the conversation between Jesus and the demons, which ends with the demons' departure into the pigs. The pigs' sudden mass suicide, the hearers' flight, the man's totally altered state, and the resulting fear of the onlookers serve as the undeniable proof of the cure.

In one respect, however, Mark seems to have altered the story. In Mark's account, Jesus' actual words of exorcism are almost an aside. The demons plead with Jesus not to torment them, and then Mark adds almost as an afterthought, "for Jesus was saying, 'Unclean spirit, come out of the person.'" Presumably, in the story Mark heard, Jesus first commanded the demons to depart, and in response, they begged him not to torture them.

By making the actual exorcism an aside, Mark continues the theme that Jesus silences demons who reveal he is God's Son. Thanks to Mark's rearrangement, we read about Jesus commanding the demons to leave immediately after they address him as "Son of the God Most High" and beg him not to torture them. Hence, now the exorcism is simultaneously an attempt to suppress the revelation of who Jesus actually is.

In keeping with what we have seen previously, here Jesus willingly works a public miracle, because it leads to his rejection. In the story, Mark emphasizes that Jesus chooses to make the exorcism a public matter. When the story begins, Jesus and his students appear to be alone with the possessed man, so Jesus could have exorcised him without making a stir. Yet, Jesus explicitly gives the demons permission to enter the pigs and causes a public uproar. Significantly, the uproar makes people confront Jesus and ask him to leave. Of course, he complies.

Also in keeping with what we have seen, Jesus does not try to keep the miracle from being publicized after his departure, because the man who has been healed has faith. Near the conclusion of the narrative, the man wants to follow Jesus. Jesus refuses the request, but invites him to tell about the exorcism.

Like the previous story, this miracle suggests that Jesus is divine. At the end of the account, Jesus commands the man to tell his relatives "how much the 'Lord' [i.e., God] has done for you." However, Mark then tells us that the man went away and proclaimed "how much Jesus had done for him." Mark invites the reader to equate Jesus with God.

Questions for Reflection:

> Does a miracle raise fundamental questions about what is real and what is truly important? Can such questions make people anxious? Does it matter whether the person who proclaims that a miracle has taken place has faith?

17.   Mark 5:21–43

And when Jesus had crossed back over to the other side, a great crowd gathered round him, and he was by the sea. And one of the leaders of the synagogue, Jairus by name, came, and when he saw him, he fell at his feet and begged him much by saying, "My little daughter is dying; so come and lay your hands on her so she may be preserved and live." And he went away with him (5:21–24a).

And a great crowd was following him, and they squeezed against him. Now there was a woman who had had a hemorrhage for twelve years. And she had suffered much with many doctors and had spent all she had and had gotten no benefit but rather had become worse. After she heard about Jesus, she came in the crowd and touched his clothes from behind, for she was saying, "If I touch even his clothes, I will be saved." And at once her bleeding dried up, and she knew from her body that she was cured of the ailment. And at once Jesus perceiving in himself that power had gone out from him turned in the crowd and said, "Who touched my clothes?" And his students said to him, "You see the crowd squeezing against you and you say, 'Who touched me?'" And he kept looking around to see the person who had done this. And the

woman, although she was afraid and shaking because she knew
what had happened to her, came and fell down before him and
told him the whole truth. But he said to her, "Daughter, your faith
has saved you. Go off in peace and be well from your ailment"
(5:24b–34).

While he was still speaking, some people came from the leader of
the synagogue's house and said, "Your daughter has died. Why
bother the teacher any longer?" But Jesus, ignoring what had been
spoken, said to the leader of the synagogue, "Don't be afraid; only
believe!" And he did not let anyone follow along with him, except
for Peter and James and John, James's brother. And they came
into the house of the leader of the synagogue, and he observed an
uproar, people weeping and wailing loudly. And when he had gone
inside, he said to them, "Why are you in an uproar and weeping?
The child has not died but is sleeping." And they jeered at him. But
he threw them all out and took along the child's father and mother
and those who were with him, and he went in where the child was.
And grasping the child's hand, he said to her, "Talitha Koum,"
which is translated, "Girl, I say to you, get up!" And at once the
girl rose and walked, for she was twelve years old. And they were
beside themselves with utter astonishment. And he strictly ordered
them that no one should know this, and he told them to give her
something to eat (5:35–43).

M ark himself probably sandwiched together the stories of
the healing of the woman with a hemorrhage and the
raising of Jairus's daughter and so wanted the reader to compare them. The oral tradition would have had difficulty remembering and repeating such a complicated structure. Instead,
early Christians would naturally have told these stories separately. These tales have very different theological emphases;
consequently, people would have used them to illustrate different points. By sandwiching these narratives, Mark invites us to
look at them together and compare and contrast them.

In the story of the hemorrhaging woman, Jesus insists on
publicizing a miracle which otherwise would have remained

secret. The narrative emphasizes that initially none of the bystanders notice that anything has happened. A "great crowd" is squeezing Jesus, and, when the woman manages to elbow her way through and touches him from behind, no one but Jesus notices. Indeed, when Jesus insists someone has touched him, his disciples respond with incredulity. Of course, lots of people have touched him! Since the woman was suffering from hemorrhaging, there is no visible evidence of the healing. Indeed, Mark explicitly tells us that "she knew from her body" she had been cured. Moreover, the narrative suggests that the woman would have kept the matter quiet. Her illness was an embarrassing one. According to biblical law, it rendered both her and whatever she touched unclean (Lev 15:25–27), and perhaps Mark and his readers knew this. Therefore, only with reluctance does she admit what has happened. Yet, Jesus insists on bringing the matter to public attention. He looks around and asks who touched him. He invites the woman to come forward, even though she is "afraid and shaking," and has her declare before everyone "the whole truth."

By contrast, in the story of the healing of Jairus's daughter, Jesus attempts to hush up a miracle which in reality could not possibly escape public notice. In telling the story, Mark emphasizes that the child's sickness and subsequent death are widely known. When the leader of the synagogue comes to Jesus to ask for help, a "great crowd" is present, and it accompanies Jesus as he starts toward the leader's home. Fresh news arrives that the girl is now dead. Once Jesus gets to the house, he meets still other people. They, too, know the girl is dead and are weeping. There is no way that the girl's miraculous raising from the dead could have been kept quiet. Just what are the child's parents supposed to say when the girl sees her friends again? Yet, in the story, Jesus does everything in his power to keep the miracle secret. When he receives the news that the girl has just died, he does not let anyone accompany him, except Peter, James, and John. When he arrives at the leader's house, he tells the mourners the girl is not dead but asleep, and when they respond with derision, he throws them out. He takes with him only the girl's parents and his chosen students. After he raises the girl from the dead, he insists that no one else should know.

The story of the healing of the hemorrhaging woman emphasizes the presence of faith, whereas the surrounding story of the raising of Jairus's daughter emphasizes its absence. In the first story, the woman has absolute confidence in Jesus' ability to heal her. Indeed, she tells herself, "If I touch even his clothes, I will be saved." After she does touch his clothes and is healed, Jesus declares, "Daughter, your faith has saved you." Significantly, the woman also shows her faith by overcoming her fear and confessing what Jesus has done for her. Even though she is "afraid and shaking," she falls down before Jesus and publicly declares the truth. By contrast, in the second story, the friends and relatives of the dead girl have no faith in Jesus' power to raise her from the dead. As soon as the girl dies, they send word to the girl's father that now Jesus should not bother to come. Not surprisingly, Jesus responds by urging him to have faith. Then when Jesus arrives at the house and suggests that the girl will be all right, everyone jeers at him. When Jesus does restore the girl to life, the few witnesses who actually see the miracle are "beside themselves with utter astonishment."

Consequently, in this section, Mark continues the theme that Jesus willingly works public miracles in response to prior faith, but he refuses to work miracles to inspire public support.

By raising Jairus's daughter, Jesus also continues to teach his disciples that they must endure and continues to hint to them who he is. Despite the fact that Jesus tries to keep the miracle from becoming public knowledge, he deliberately works it in the presence of Peter, James, and John. Jesus explicitly lets them come along to the house and go in to "where the child was." Of course, the story teaches the need to trust in Jesus despite disappointment and seeming hopelessness. After the father invites Jesus to heal his daughter, she dies and everyone despairs. By raising her Jesus reveals that he has divine power for only God can give life to the dead.

Questions for Reflection:

> Do small miracles (or even big ones) happen frequently, but people are afraid to disclose them? If so, what is the source of this fear? It is always a good idea to tell people about a miracle?

18.   Mark 6:1-6a

And he went away from there and came into his hometown, and his students followed him. And when it was the Sabbath, he began to teach in the synagogue, and many who heard him were astonished and said, "Where did he get this from, and what is the wisdom which has been given to him? And such miracles happen at his hands! Is not this the carpenter, the son of Mary and brother of James and Joses and Jude and Simon? And are not his sisters here with us?" And they were scandalized at him. And Jesus said to them, "A prophet is not dishonored, except in his hometown and among his kin and in his house." And he could not do any miracle there, except that he laid his hands on a few sick and healed them. And he marveled because of their lack of faith (6:1-6a).

This section borders on being inconsistent. Mark first emphasizes that Jesus could not do any miracle. But then he adds that Jesus did in fact heal some sick people.

I suspect this tension arose when Mark edited an earlier tradition. That tradition reported that Jesus went to his hometown, healed some sick people, but nevertheless got a cool reception. His relatives and childhood friends could not believe he was anyone special.

Mark reshaped the material so that it would be consistent with his theme that Jesus did not work miracles to impress skeptics. Mark played down the miracles that Jesus did work by saying that he healed only a few. Instead, Mark emphasized that the lack of faith made it impossible for Jesus to do wonders.

Thanks to the reshaping, this brief section makes explicit the point that the previous section implied. Earlier we saw that the interlocking stories of the hemorrhaging woman and the raising of Jairus's daughter clearly imply that Jesus works public miracles in response to faith, but refuses to work miracles to produce it. Now in the following section, Mark explicitly states that Jesus could not work miracles due to the lack of faith which the people of Nazareth displayed.

The passage also introduces a new and disturbing theme, namely that lack of faith undermines Jesus' own power. Earlier in the gospel, lack of faith does not diminish Jesus' ability to do wonders. It merely makes him try to keep them from coming to public attention. Mark will return later to the theme that unbelief reduces Jesus' capacity to work miracles.

The section reinforces the point that Jesus' students are his true family. Earlier, his natural mother and siblings tried to seize him, and Jesus declared that those who do God's will are his true mother and brothers and sisters (3:20–35). Now we read that Jesus had no honor "in his hometown and among his kin and in his house." Significantly, in the following verses Jesus shares his authority and mission with the twelve.

Questions for Reflection:

If it is God who performs miracles, why does lack of faith make them more difficult? Why do we notice prophets and saints who are far away much more easily than prophets and saints who arise from our own midst? Does the particular community in which I live have any?

19.   Mark 6:6b-30

And he went about among the villages teaching. And he summoned the twelve and began to send them out two by two, and he gave them authority over unclean spirits, and he directed them to take nothing on the road, except a walking stick only, no bread, no knapsack, no copper coins in their belt. But they were to wear sandals. "And do not put on two sets of clothes!" And he said to them, "Whenever you go into a house, remain there until you leave from there. And whatever place does not receive you and does not listen to you, when you go out from there, shake off the dust from the bottom of your feet for a testimony to them." And they went out and proclaimed that people should repent, and they drove out many demons, and anointed with oil many sick and healed them (6:6b–13).

And King Herod heard of it for his name became known, and people were saying that John the Baptizer had been raised from the dead and that was the reason these powers were at work in him. And others were saying that it was Elijah. And still others were saying that it was a prophet like one of the prophets of old. But Herod when he heard was saying, "John whom I beheaded has been raised." For Herod himself had sent and seized John and put him bound in prison because of Herodias, his brother Philip's wife, because Herod married her, for John was saying to Herod, "It is not allowed for you to have your brother's wife." And Herodias had it in for him and wanted to kill him; yet she could not for Herod was afraid of John, since he knew he was a righteous and holy man. And he protected him. And when he listened to him, he was utterly at a loss, yet he listened to him gladly. And after an opportune day arrived, when Herod for his birthday festivities gave a banquet for his courtiers and generals and the leaders of Galilee, his daughter by Herodias came in and danced and pleased Herod and those who were dining with him. The king said to the girl, "Ask me for whatever you want, and I will give it to you." And he swore to her vehemently, "Whatever at all you ask me, I will give to you up to half of my kingdom." And she went out and said to her mother, "What shall I ask for?" And she said, "The head of John the Baptizer!" And she at once went in with haste to the king and asked, "I want you immediately to give me on a plate the head of John the Baptist." And although the king was greatly grieved, he did not want to refuse her because of the oaths and those who were dining. And at once the king sent out an executioner with the order to bring his head. And he went away and beheaded him in prison and brought his head on a plate and gave it to the girl, and the girl gave it to her mother. And when his students heard, they came and took away his corpse and put it in a tomb (6:14–29).

And the missionaries gathered by Jesus and reported to him all they had done and all they had taught (6:30).

Here again, Mark has sandwiched together two independent stories. In the oral tradition, the stories of the mission of the twelve and of the execution of John the Baptist were surely told separately, since in every respect they differ. Yet, Mark has combined them.

By juxtaposing these stories, Mark is inviting us to compare two different kinds of discipleship. First, we have the discipleship of the twelve, which consists of voluntary poverty, preaching repentance, and working miracles. Then, we have the discipleship of John, which consists of suffering imprisonment and grisly death.

Mark suggests that the first kind of discipleship is a genuine expression of faith in Jesus. In the immediately preceding story the people of Nazareth have no faith, and Jesus cannot work miracles. Now the disciples are able to heal the sick. Consequently, Jesus is able to send them on a mission, and that mission expresses their genuine trust in him.

The second kind of discipleship, however, involves a much deeper identification with Jesus. The narrative suggests that thanks to his sufferings, John is the very image of Jesus. Indeed, in the story, Herod declares that Jesus is John the Baptist raised from the dead. Of course, John's execution by Herod foreshadows Jesus' crucifixion by Pilate. Later Jesus too will be "seized" (14:46) and "bound" (15:1). Other passages in the gospel also make John's teaching and suffering a symbol for those of Jesus himself (e.g., 9:11–13).

This section taken as a whole continues Mark's theme that the twelve already have a special relationship to Jesus, but still have to learn that they must suffer. Like Jesus, they preach and heal, but unlike Jesus and John they are not yet ready to die.

Because the disciples have not learned they must suffer, it is not yet time to preach the good news to the world. Therefore, when they go out, they do not proclaim that Jesus is Lord or even that God's rule has come. Instead, they preach only that "people should repent." As Mark's treatment of the Parable of the Sower suggested, it is still the period of preparation.

Questions for Reflection:

Do many people who have a genuine relationship with Jesus still have to learn that they must suffer with him? When such people talk about Christianity, what can they convincingly proclaim? What are they not able to proclaim until they have suffered?

20.   Mark 6:31–52

And he said to them, "You come by yourselves into an uninhabited place and rest a little." For many were coming and going, and they did not even have an opportunity to eat. And they went away in the boat to an uninhabited place by themselves. Yet many saw them going off and recognized them. And by land from all the cities they ran together there, and they arrived before them. And when he got out, he saw a great crowd, and he had compassion on them, because they were like sheep which do not have a shepherd, and he began to teach them many things. And when the hour had already become late, his students came to him and said, "This is an uninhabited place and the hour already late. Send them away that they may go away into the surrounding fields and villages and buy for themselves something they can eat." But in reply he said to them, "You give them something to eat." And they said to him, "Shall we go away and buy two hundred days' wages of bread and give them to eat?" But he said to them, "How many loaves do you have? Go off, see." And when they knew, they said, "Five, and two fish." And he ordered them to seat everyone group by group on the green grass. And they got down section by section, by hundreds and by fifties. And taking the five loaves and the two fish, he looked up into heaven and blessed and broke up the loaves and kept giving them to his students, so they might set them before them, and he distributed the two fish to all. And all ate and were filled. And they took up twelve wicker baskets full of crumbs and of pieces of fish. And those who ate the loaves were five thousand men (6:31–44).

And at once he made his students get into the boat and go ahead across to Bethsaida, while he dismissed the crowd himself. And after saying farewell to them, he went off to the mountain to pray. And when it had become evening, the boat was in the middle of the sea, and he alone on the land. And after he saw they were distressed in rowing for the wind was against them, about the fourth watch of the night he came to them walking on the sea, and he intended to pass by them. But when they saw him walking on the sea, they thought that it was a ghost, and they cried out. For they all saw him and were alarmed. But at once he spoke with them and said to them, "Take courage, it is I; do not be afraid." And he came up to them into the boat, and the wind stopped, and they were utterly beside themselves, for they did not understand about the loaves, but their mind was closed (6:45–52).

Mark explicitly tells the reader that these two stories should be seen together because they make the same point. The end of the second story, "for they did not understand about the loaves, but their mind was closed," refers back to the first and suggests that Jesus' students have twice failed to grasp the point. Accordingly, Mark challenges the reader to perceive the truth that eludes the disciples.

The point that the disciples fail to grasp is a teaching which should now be familiar to the reader, namely the disciples should trust Jesus because he exercises the very power of God. Thus, in both stories Jesus exercises divine prerogatives. In the first story, Jesus gives the people bread in the wilderness, and so this miracle recalls God giving the people of Israel manna in the desert (e.g., Exod 16:14–15). In the second story, Jesus walks on water, and in the Hebrew Scriptures, God alone walks on the waters (Job 9:8, 38:16). Lest we miss the point, Mark gives us other signs of Jesus' divinity. The story tells us that Jesus meant to "pass by," and in theophanies in the Hebrew Scriptures God reveals himself while passing by (Exod 33:18–23, 1 Kgs 19:11). Then, when the disciples become fearful in the presence of divine power, Jesus declares, "It is I." In Greek, these words are literally, "I am," and they recall the scene in Exodus 3 when Moses asks God what his name is, and God replies, "I am who I am" (Exod 3:14).

In both stories, Jesus also challenges his students to persevere in seemingly hopeless situations. In the first narrative, when the disciples tell Jesus to send the crowd away to buy food, he challenges them to give the people something to eat. When they object that two hundred days' wages of bread would be necessary, he forces them to see that they have only five loaves and two fish. He tells them to seat the crowd. Only at this point does he multiply the bread and fish so that the disciples can feed everyone. In the second narrative, Jesus again sends the disciples into a difficult situation. He makes "his students get into the boat and go ahead" without him. When they reach the middle of the lake, they are stymied because the wind is against them. Even though they are straining at the oars, they go nowhere. Apparently, Jesus intends to test them further, because he means to "pass by" rather than end their difficulties.

Accordingly, these stories continue the themes which first come up in the account of the stilling of the storm (4:35–41). There, too, Jesus challenges the disciples to persevere and reveals his divine power. When the storm is sinking the boat, he is asleep. When they panic and awake him, he reveals his divine power by calming the elements. In that story, too, the disciples fail to understand. Mark's readers need to do better.

We may note that, as we would expect, Jesus works these two miracles in private because there is no prior faith and they would lead to public acclaim if they became known. Thus, as soon as he feeds the crowds, Jesus makes the disciples leave and sends the crowds away. Such measures are necessary to keep the multitude from discovering that Jesus multiplied the loaves and fish. So too, when Jesus walks on water, only his students are present to see.

The two miracles, also introduce a major new theme, namely that miracles do not produce genuine faith. After they saw Jesus feed five thousand men with five loaves of bread, the disciples might reasonably have concluded that Jesus could do anything. However, immediately thereafter when they see Jesus walking on water and exercising control over the wind, his students "were utterly beside themselves." The point is evident: Even though faith produces miracles, miracles do not produce faith. As we shall see, this theme will keep recurring right through to the crucifixion.

Questions for Reflection:

Does Jesus sometimes call us to persevere in seemingly hopeless situations? How can we distinguish this call from mere wishful thinking that tells us that everything will always turn out all right? What kind of faith do miracles inspire? Is such faith enough?

21. Mark 6:53-56

And crossing over to the land, they came to Gennesaret and beached. And as they were coming out of the boat, at once people recognized him, and they ran around that whole district and began to bring around on cots those who were sick where they heard that he was. And wherever he went into villages or into cities or into the countryside, they would put those who were infirm in the marketplaces and beg him that they might touch even the edge of his garment, and all who touched him were saved (6:53–56).

In this brief section Mark emphasizes that Jesus worked many public miracles. The crowds lay large numbers of infirm people in the marketplaces, and Jesus heals them all.

Jesus performs these public miracles in response to persistent faith. Earlier in the gospel, Jesus sees the faith of the four men who lug the paralytic on a cot up onto the roof (2:3–5), and Jesus commends the faith of the woman with the hemorrhage who wishes to touch just his clothes (5:25–34, especially vs. 28). If anything, the people in this passage have an even greater faith. They lug "around on cots those who were sick where they heard that he was," and beg to "touch even the edge of his garment"—such is their persistence in seeking him out and following him, and their confidence in his power.

Questions for Reflection:

Do people who have faith seek for miracles in a different
way from people who lack it? What are the differences and
are they important?

22.   Mark 7:1-30

*And the Pharisees and some of the scribes who had come from
Jerusalem gathered by him. And they saw that some of his students
were eating bread with defiled hands, (that is unwashed)—for
Pharisees and all the Jews do not eat unless they wash their hands
to the wrist, since they keep the tradition of the elders, and when
they come from the marketplace, they do not eat unless they wash,
and there are many other things which they accept and keep, the
washing of cups and pitchers and kettles—and the Pharisees and
scribes asked him, "Why don't your students walk in accordance
with the tradition of the elders, but eat bread with defiled hands?"
But he said to them, "Well did Isaiah prophesy about you hypo-
crites, as it is written, 'This people honors me with their lips, but
their heart is far away from me. In vain they worship me, since they
teach human commandments.' Forsaking God's commandment,
you hold on to human tradition." And he said to them, "You have
a fine way of rejecting God's commandment to establish your
tradition! For Moses said, 'Honor your father and your mother,'
and, 'Whoever reviles father or mother shall surely die.' But you
say, 'If a person says to father or mother, "Corban" (that is,
whatever you would have profited from me is a "gift"), you no
longer let them do anything for father or mother. You invalidate
God's word by your tradition which you hand on; and you do many
such similar things!" (7:1–13).*

And he summoned the crowd back and said to them, "Listen to me, all of you, and understand! There is nothing from outside which can defile by going into a person, but the things which come out of a person are what defile them." And when he went into a house away from the crowd, his students asked him about the figure of speech. And he said to them, "So are you too without understanding? Do you not realize that nothing that goes into a person from outside can defile them? Because it does not go into their heart but into their stomach and goes out into the toilet." (He was declaring that all foods are clean.) And he said, "What comes out of a person, that defiles the person. For from within, from people's heart, come wicked doubts, fornications, thefts, murders, adulteries, greed, maliciousness, deceit, debauchery, an evil eye, slander, arrogance, foolishness; all these wicked things come out from within and defile a person" (7:14–23).

And he rose and went away from there into the territory of Tyre and went into a house, and he did not want anyone to know, yet he could not be hidden. But at once a woman whose little daughter had an unclean spirit heard about him and came and fell at his feet. Now the woman was a Gentile, a Syrophoenician by nationality. And she kept asking him to drive out the demon from her daughter. And he said to her, "Let the children first be fed, for it is not good to take the children's bread and throw it to the dogs." But she said to him in reply, "Sir, even the dogs under the table eat from the children's crumbs." And he said to her, "On account of this saying, go, the demon has departed from your daughter." And she went away to her house and found the child lying on the bed and the demon gone (7:24–30).

At first glance these two pieces of tradition have little in common. Jesus' dispute with the Pharisees concerning eating with defiled hands seems unrelated to Jesus performing an exorcism in response to the urging of a foreign woman.

Mark's version of the confrontation with the Pharisees makes it clear he was writing primarily for Gentiles. Not only does Mark interrupt the traditional narrative to explain that "defiled" means "unwashed," but he also goes on to detail a host of other customs which he apparently thought "all the Jews" keep.

Because he was writing for Gentiles, Mark must have felt the story of the Syrophoenician woman needed careful handling. His readers might easily take offense at Jesus calling Gentiles "dogs" and initially refusing to aid a Gentile woman. Moreover, they might also conclude that Jesus' message was not really for them. Significantly, Mark carefully includes the word *first* in Jesus' statement about feeding the children and thus makes it clear that Jesus always envisioned that his message would reach the pagans in due course.

By juxtaposing the two pieces of tradition, Mark stresses to his readers that Jesus did not consider the Gentile woman or Gentile food to be dirty. In the debate between Jesus and the Pharisees, Jesus insists that externals do not make someone unclean. There is nothing from outside that defiles a person, and then Mark makes the parenthetical comment that, therefore, "all foods are clean." The gospel emphasizes that this message is for the reader by having Jesus summon the crowd and challenge them *all* to understand.

The Gentile woman was justified by her persistent faith. In the debate between Jesus and the Pharisees, Jesus insists that the only thing that can defile a person is what comes from the heart. Subsequently, Jesus challenges the Gentile woman, and she replies by showing both humility and persistent trust. In the presence of Jesus, she modestly accepts his criticism that she is a "dog," yet she persists in pressing her request. Jesus then grants it and notes that he does so because of what she has just said. Significantly, Jesus merely assures the woman that the demon has left her daughter. Initially, there is no proof. It is because of her great faith in Jesus' power and truthfulness that the woman can accept his word and depart. Only then does she gain confirmation that the exorcism has indeed taken place.

By contrast, Mark suggests that lack of faith defiles the Pharisees. Outwardly, they maintain the highest standard of cleanliness. Indeed, Mark implies they go too far! However, they are utterly hypocritical and wicked. Significantly, at the end of the story we have a list of vices, and the first and the last both suggest stupid unbelief. Thus, the list begins with "wicked doubts" and ends with "foolishness." The real error of the Pharisees is that they do not believe in Jesus.

Once again, Jesus does not hesitate to work a miracle for someone who is not a disciple once the outsider has shown she has faith. At the beginning of the story about the Syrophoenician woman, Jesus is trying to hide. When the woman finds him, he initially refuses to work a miracle. Then, however, the woman, by her persistence in pressing her request, shows she truly believes in Jesus. Hence, he works the miracle, and, as we would expect from previous stories, Jesus does not ask the woman to keep the matter secret.

This section continues the theme that Jesus' students are failing to grasp his message and so are becoming no better than outsiders. Jesus' public teaching about true purity seems clear, and he apparently expects the crowd to be able to grasp it. Indeed, he issues the challenge, "Listen to me, all of you, and understand!" Yet, the disciples must privately ask for clarification. Before giving it, Jesus underlines their lack of comprehension. "So are you too without understanding?"

Questions for Reflection:

Do religious people today still sometimes assume that externals are what make someone unclean? What are some examples of such externals? What makes someone's inner self clean or unclean?

23.   Mark 7:31–37

And he came back out of the territory of Tyre and came through Sidon to the Sea of Galilee in the middle of the territory of the Decapolis. And they brought to him a man who was deaf and speech-impaired and begged him to lay his hand on him. And he took him aside, away from the crowd, and privately he thrust his fingers into his ears and spat and touched his tongue, and looking up into heaven, he groaned and said to him, "Ephphatha," that is, "Be opened up!" And at once, his hearing was opened, and the bond of his tongue was undone, and he spoke normally. And he ordered them to talk to no one. Yet the more he ordered them, the more abundantly they proclaimed it. And they were utterly astounded and said, "He has done all things well. He both makes the deaf to hear and the mute to speak" (7:31–37).

This story suffers from a major inconsistency, which probably is due to Mark himself. In the narrative, Jesus works the miracle after taking the deaf man "aside"; yet we then read, "He ordered them to talk to no one." Who this "them" is remains unclear. Since the command to talk to no one is an ongoing theme in this gospel, we may suppose that Mark added it and so produced the contradiction.

Because of the inconsistency, Mark is able to stress both that Jesus worked the miracle in private and that the public acclaimed him. Indeed, Mark makes both points emphatically. Jesus "took him aside, away from the crowd, and privately he thrust his fingers into his ears." "And they were utterly astounded and said, 'He has done all things well.'"

This story once again makes the point that Jesus tries to hide miracles when there is no faith or when the miracle itself produces public acclaim. In the narrative, Mark emphasizes Jesus' attempts to hush up the miracle. Not only does Jesus deliberately work the miracle in private; in addition, he orders people "to talk to no one." Nevertheless, they break faith with him utterly. "The more he ordered them" not to talk about what happened, the more they proclaim it. The news, as it spreads, produces not faith, but astonishment, and with the astonishment comes public acclaim.

Nevertheless, the story introduces a new theme, namely, that Jesus' miracles are beginning to diminish due to the persistent lack of faith. Earlier we noted that this theme is foreshadowed in Jesus' inability to do many miracles at Nazareth when his childhood acquaintances dismiss him as no one special (6:1–6). Now we have the beginning of a sustained presentation. From here on, with only one exception, Jesus either will have more difficulty performing the miracles or the miracles will be less spectacular—or both. In this opening story, Jesus has to strain to accomplish the healing. Whereas in the previous narrative, Jesus heals the Syrophoenician woman's daughter effortlessly and at a distance, now he must thrust his fingers into the man's ears, touch his tongue with saliva, and utter the mysterious word, *Ephphatha*. The miracle apparently also involves inner struggle. Jesus looks into heaven and groans.

Questions for Reflection:

What is the difference between a Christian faith healer and a successful psychic healer or even a charlatan? Would someone who lacks faith and hears about a Christian healer be in a postion to grasp the difference? Do you think that many of the people who heard about Jesus' miracles mistook him for a sorcerer? If so, would they have tried to become his followers? What would Jesus have said to such people?

24.   Mark 8:1–21

In those days when there was again a great crowd and they did not have anything to eat, he summoned the students and said to them, "I have compassion on the crowd, because they have already stayed with me three days, and they do not have anything to eat. And if I send them away to their homes hungry, they will become faint on the road. And some of them have come from far away." And his students answered him, "From where will anyone be able to satisfy these people with bread here in the uninhabited land?" And he asked them, "How many loaves of bread do you have?" And they said, "Seven." And he ordered the crowd to get down on the ground. And he took the seven loaves and gave thanks and broke them and kept giving them to his students to set them out, and they set them before the crowd. And they had a few fish. And he blessed them and said that these too were to be set out. And they ate and were satisfied, and they took up seven mat baskets of leftover crumbs. And there were about four thousand people. And he dismissed them. And at once he got into the boat with his students and came to the region of Dalmanoutha (8:1–10).

And the Pharisees came out and began to argue with him and seek from him a sign from heaven to test him. And groaning intensely in his spirit he said, "Why does this generation seek a sign? Truly I say to you, I swear no sign will be given to this generation!" And he left them and got back into the boat and went away to the other side (8:11–13).

And they forgot to take bread, and, except for one loaf, they did not have any with them in the boat. And he commanded them, "Look out, watch out for the leaven of the Pharisees and the leaven of Herod." And they discussed with one another that they did not have any bread. And when he knew, he said to them, "Why are you discussing that you do not have any bread? Do you not yet comprehend or understand? Do you have your mind closed? Having eyes, do you not see, and having ears, do you not hear? And do you not recall? When I broke the five loaves for the five thousand, how many wicker baskets full of crumbs did you take up?" They said to him, "Twelve." "When the seven for the four thousand, how many mat baskets of crumbs did you take up full?" And they said, "Seven." And he kept saying to them, "Do you not yet understand?" (8:14–21)

It is striking that Mark chose to tell the story of the feeding of the multitude twice. Naturally, it is conceivable that Jesus worked such a miracle more than once. Even if he did so, however, the oral tradition would have had difficulty keeping such similar incidents separate, and, in any event, an evangelist was under no obligation to record everything Jesus did. What is perhaps more likely, however, is that Jesus only did the miracle once, and the oral tradition was not entirely consistent on such numbers as how many people Jesus fed with how many loaves of bread. Luke, even though he uses Mark, records only one such feeding (Luke 9:10–17). John, who may have worked independently, does the same (John 6:1–13).[1]

Mark suggests that the numerical details in the feedings have a tremendous significance and challenges the reader to figure out what it is. In 8:17–18, Jesus berates his disciples for obtuseness. They have eyes and yet do not see, and ears and yet do not hear. This rebuke is all the more stinging because it echoes the description in 4:12 of outsiders. The disciples are no better than outsiders! Then Jesus reminds the disciples of the exact numbers in the feedings. The first time, he broke five loaves and fed five thousand people; twelve baskets of crumbs were left. By contrast, the second time, he broke seven loaves and fed four thousand people; and seven baskets of crumbs were left. Then Jesus asks in amazement whether the disciples still do not understand. Such attacks on the disciples, of course, put pressure on the reader. We certainly do not wish to share in Jesus' condemnation!

As Countryman has argued,[2] the point of the numbers is that Jesus' miracles are decreasing. In the first miracle, Jesus started with less bread, fed more people, and more was left over. Therefore, the second feeding was in every respect inferior.[3]

Of course, the reason for the decline is the continuing lack of faith. One is tempted to write the increasing lack of faith. After Jesus feeds the five thousand, the disciples surely should realize he can do a similar miracle. Yet, when the story of the second feeding begins, Jesus points out once again that the crowd needs to eat, and the disciples respond by saying that no one could feed such a mob. When Jesus repeats the miracle, his students still learn nothing. Only a few verses later, they are alone with Jesus and become concerned that they have only one loaf of bread!

Not surprisingly, Mark emphasizes in this context that even though faith produces miracles, miracles do not produce real faith. Just after he feeds the four thousand, the Pharisees tempt Jesus by asking him to work a miraculous sign. Jesus refuses. He then warns his students to beware of the "leaven of the Pharisees and the leaven of Herod." Clearly, the leaven of the Pharisees is demanding miracles as a precondition for faith. Of course, the faith which would result from such demonstrations would be incompatible with that trust in Jesus which perseveres in following him despite difficulties. Apparently, Herod too has this inferior type of faith. The only other Markan passage in which Herod's name appears is 6:14–29. There, Herod orders the execution of John the Baptist, and then, when he hears that Jesus is working miracles, Herod assumes Jesus is John raised from the dead. Jesus' miracles have produced some sort of faith in Herod—but not persevering trust in him.

Questions for Reflection:

Where does genuine faith in God and in Jesus come from? Can we get true faith by demanding that God or Jesus do something for us first, such as work a miraculous sign?

25.   Mark 8:22–26

And they came to Bethsaida. And they brought to him a blind man and begged him to touch him. And after he had grasped the blind man's hand, he led him out of the village. And he spat into his eyes ʾ laid his hands on him and asked him, "Do you see anything?" looking up he said, "I see people, but they look like walking " Then he laid his hands on his eyes again, and he looked ly, and he was cured and saw everything clearly. And he sent ʾ his house by saying, "Do not even go into the village!" (8:22–26).

Just as Mark invites us to connect the feeding of the four thousand with the earlier feeding of the five, so here he apparently wants us to connect this story with that of the healing of the man who was deaf and dumb (7:32–37). There are many parallels between them. The content of the two stories is similar. Most strikingly, these are the only narratives in Mark in which Jesus employs saliva. The wording is also similar. For example, both stories begin, "And they brought to him . . . and begged him to. . . ."

In connection with the earlier healing, this passage admirably continues the two themes Mark has been developing about miracles. Once again, Jesus tries to keep the public from learning about a miracle where there is no faith. In the story, we get no indication that anyone has any real belief in Jesus. Consequently, Jesus takes the man outside the village and heals him in private. Then he orders him not to return to the village. Of course, the story also illustrates in an especially dramatic way that the lack of faith is reducing Jesus' ability to work miracles. Not only, as in the earlier story, must Jesus employ saliva and the laying on of hands. Now, he must take two tries. After the first attempt, the man's sight is still so poor that people look like walking trees.

Nevertheless, the passage also prepares us for the two related stories that will follow. In the next narrative, Peter confesses that Jesus is the Messiah, but objects when Jesus declares that he and his students must suffer. In the following story, a voice from heaven declares that Jesus is God's Son, and subsequently Jesus again tells his students that he must suffer. Accordingly, the two-stage healing of the blind man symbolizes the two-stage confession which will follow immediately. When Peter confesses that Jesus is the Messiah but denies the need to suffer, Peter is beginning to see, but his limited sight is comparable to being unable to distinguish between human beings and walking trees. True sight is to perceive that Jesus is God's Son and that he and we must suffer. Significantly, just before the story of the healing of the blind man, Mark uses *sight* figuratively, and so prepares us to interpret the story symbolically. In 8:18, Jesus berates the disciples for their spiritual obtuseness by noting that even though they have eyes they do not "see."

Questions for Reflection:

In general, is it harder to help someone who lacks trust? Why? Do some people today confess that Jesus is the Messiah and yet assume that, thanks to Jesus, they will not have to suffer? Is such faith realistic? Is it Christian?

26.   Mark 8:27 - 9:13

And Jesus and his students went out into the villages of Caesarea Philippi. And on the road he kept asking his students, saying to them, "Who do people say that I am?" And they said to him, "John the Baptist; yet others say, Elijah, and others, one of the Prophets."

And he asked them, "But you, who do you say that I am?" In Peter said to him, "You are the Messiah!" (8:27–29).

And he reprimanded them so they would not speak to anyo. about him. And he began to teach them that the son of humanity had to suffer much and be rejected by the elders and the chief priests and the scribes and be killed and after three days rise. And he spoke the message openly. And Peter took him aside and began to reprimand him. But after he turned and saw his students, he reprimanded Peter and said, "Get out of my sight, Satan, because you are not thinking about the things of God but of human beings" (8:30–33).

And he summoned the crowd along with his students and said to them, "If anyone wants to follow after me, let them deny themself and take up their cross and follow me. For whoever wants to save their life will lose it, but whoever will lose their life because of the good news will save it. For how will it benefit a person to gain the whole world and forfeit their life? For what would a person give as an exchange for their life? For whoever is ashamed of me and my words in this adulterous and sinful generation, the son of humanity will also be ashamed of them when he comes in his Father's glory with the holy angels." And he said to them, "Truly I say to you that there are some of those standing here who will not taste of death until they see God's rule has come in power" (8:34–9:1).

And after six days Jesus took along Peter and James and John and brought them up on a high mountain privately by themselves. And he was transformed before them, and his clothes became shining, very white, as no launderer on earth could bleach. And there appeared to them Elijah with Moses, and they were talking together with Jesus. And in response Peter said to Jesus, "Rabbi, it is good that we are here, and let us make three booths, one for you and one for Moses and one for Elijah." For he did not know what to respond, for they had become terrified. And a cloud covered them, and there was a voice from the cloud, "This is my beloved Son, listen to him!" And suddenly, when they looked around, they no longer saw anyone with them but Jesus only. And as they were coming down from the mountain, he ordered them to tell no one what they saw until the son of humanity rose from the dead. And they kept the matter to themselves, discussing what rising from the dead was. And they asked him, "The scribes say that Elijah must come first?" And he said to them, "Elijah is coming first and is going to restore all things; and how is it written about the son of humanity that he must suffer much and be despised? But I tell you that, nevertheless, Elijah has come, and they did to him whatever they wanted, just as it is written about him" (9:2–13).

Mark invites the reader[4] to view Peter's confession and the transfiguration together. The preface to the second narrative tells us that the transfiguration happened six days later and so connects the two stories. Moreover, the prophecy at the end of the first story that people will soon see "God's rule has come in power" points to the second. The vision of Jesus in shining garments and talking with Moses and Elijah foreshadows the coming kingdom.

Mark emphasizes that this combined section is important by repeating in it the themes and even the actual words of the opening verses of the gospel. Thus, the gospel begins by telling us that Jesus is the Messiah and God's Son (1:1), and now Peter confesses that Jesus is the Messiah, and God proclaims that Jesus is "my beloved Son." Of course, these words also remind the reader of Jesus' baptism when God says to Jesus, "You are my beloved Son" (1:11).

In this section, Jesus openly declares to his students for the first time that he is God's Son. Previously, Jesus tries to suppress this information. When the demons reveal who he truly is, Jesus silences them (e.g., 3:11). Then he chooses a special group of followers and begins to give them hints concerning his true identity. Now, however, Jesus tells them explicitly. He asks the disciples who they think he is and elicits Peter's response that he is the Messiah. Then he leads the inner core of his followers up the mountain. There he is transformed before them, and God himself proclaims to them that Jesus is his "beloved Son."

As God's Son, Jesus is greater than any earthly messiah. When Peter confesses that Jesus is the Messiah, he apparently assumes that Jesus is merely the most important monarch in the world. During the following scene, Peter wishes to accord the same dignity to Moses and Elijah as to Jesus. Peter offers to make a shrine for each. However, the heavenly voice corrects him. Jesus is God's Son, and the disciples must listen to him alone.

Jesus insists that the disciples must keep his identity secret until his mission of suffering has been completed. When Peter proclaims that Jesus is the Messiah, Jesus responds by insisting that Peter inform no one since Jesus must suffer. Similarly, Mark emphasizes that the transfiguration is confidential. Before the vision, Jesus takes the inner core of his followers up a mountain "privately by themselves." After the heavenly voice declares that Jesus is God's Son, Jesus insists that his followers must not share this secret until he has risen from the dead.

Accordingly, these stories bring the first half of the gospel to a climax by explaining why Jesus has tried to keep his identity secret and by summarizing what he has been trying to teach his disciples. He has tried to keep his identity secret to avoid public acclaim so he can pursue his mission to serve humbly and be rejected. He has been trying to teach his disciples that they can trust him and patiently endure because he is God's Son. Significantly, when Peter declares that Jesus is the Messiah and then objects to him suffering, Jesus dismisses him as "Satan." Previously, Satan tried to derail Jesus' mission of suffering by using the demons to declare publicly that Jesus is God's Son. Now, Satan is using Peter to accomplish the same goal.

These stories also give us a preview of the gospel's second half, which emphasizes that Jesus must suffer before being glorified and that we must imitate his example. Mark stresses that he is introducing an important new theme by saying that Jesus "began to teach them . . ." The confession of Peter is the first of three blocks of material which predict the passion, and each block has a similar structure. The structure is that Jesus first announces he must suffer, die, and rise from the dead. Then, we have a story in which the disciples demonstrate that they do not understand what Jesus really means. Finally, Jesus teaches the need for humble discipleship. In this first prediction, of course, the negative reaction by the disciples is Peter's insistence that Jesus must not suffer. Jesus then teaches that anyone who would follow him must deny themself and take up their cross. Similar themes appear near the end of the story of the transfiguration. There, Jesus points out that John the Baptist ("Elijah") has suffered already and that he himself must suffer too, but that in the end he will rise from the dead. However, Mark emphasizes that the disciples did not understand what rising from the dead meant.

Because both Jesus and his followers must suffer, he insists that he is not merely the Messiah but also the son of humanity. Peter declares Jesus is the Messiah, but objects when Jesus announces that he must suffer. Therefore, Jesus identifies himself as the "son of humanity"—that is, as a human being. As such, he will be our example and our judge. He will suffer the way that only human beings can. On the last day he will also judge us on whether we have been faithful to his example. Whoever is ashamed of him, of them Jesus will also be ashamed at the final judgment!

Significantly, Mark suggests that we only learn who Jesus is by following him, especially following him to the cross. Thus, Jesus first asks the disciples who other people say that he is. In response, we get the same rumors Herod heard in chapter 6, namely that Jesus is John the Baptist or Elijah or one of the Prophets (8:28; cf. 6:14–15). Then Jesus asks the disciples who they say he is. Because Peter has followed him and received secret instruction and seen private miracles, he is able to declare that Jesus is the Messiah. However, to know that Jesus is the Son of God, Christians must be ready to follow Jesus to the cross. Hence, the disciples apparently do not fully grasp what the heavenly voice means when it declares that Jesus is God's

Son. Instead, the disciples struggle to understand what the rising from the dead might be.

Mark makes it clear that Jesus' message of the need to suffer is for everyone—including the reader. Whereas the rest of the material in this section occurs in private, Jesus' declaration on the need to take up one's cross is public. Mark explicitly states that Jesus summoned "the crowd along with his students." Significantly, the rest of the narrative gives us no reason to think that such a crowd is in fact present. Mark suddenly introduces them here in order to stress to his reader that what Jesus is about to say is of general interest. Then Jesus speaks about "anyone" who would follow him.

Mark reminds his readers that Jesus will return soon to reward those who remain faithful. Jesus dramatically concludes his remarks in chapter 8 by insisting that some of his original audience will still be alive when "God's rule has come in power." Historically, Jesus' comment must have been somewhat ambiguous, but, as we shall see, Mark apparently took it to mean that Jesus would return in glory during the lifetime of his original followers. Of course, when Mark was writing years later, the amount of time in which this prophecy could come true had diminished considerably. Hence, Mark is reminding his readers that they will "see" Jesus in the relatively near future.

Questions for Reflection:

Who do non-Christians today say that Jesus is? How do we who follow Jesus learn that he is not merely a great human being, but God's Son? Do we in our own lives and our own communities have moments like the transfiguration when we get a foretaste of God's rule coming in power?

27.   Mark 9:14–29

And when they came to the students, they saw a great crowd around them and scribes arguing with them. And at once all the crowd saw him and were astonished, and they ran to him and greeted him. And he asked them, "What were you arguing about with them?" And one of the crowd replied to him, "Teacher, I brought my son to you, since he has a spirit which makes him mute. And wherever it seizes him, it throws him down, and he foams at the mouth and grinds his teeth and becomes rigid. And I said to your students to drive it out, and they were not able." And in reply he said to them, "O faithless generation! How long will I be with you? How long will I put up with you? Bring him to me." And they brought him to him. And when the spirit saw him, at once it convulsed him, and he fell on the ground and rolled around, foaming at the mouth. And he asked his father, "How long has he been like this?" And he said, "From childhood. And often it throws him even into fire, even into water, to kill him, but if you can do anything, have compassion on us and help us." But Jesus said to him, "'If you can!' All things are possible to one who has faith!" At once the father of the child shouted, "I believe; help my unbelief." When Jesus saw that a crowd was running together, he reprimanded the unclean spirit by saying to it, "Spirit who causes dumbness and deafness, I order you, come out of him and do not go into him anymore." And shouting and convulsing him greatly, it came out. And he became as if dead, so that many said that he had died. But Jesus grasped his hand and raised him, and he rose. And when he had gone into a house, his students asked him privately, "Why couldn't we drive it out?" And he said to them, "This type cannot be sent out by anything except prayer" (9:14–29).

I would suggest that Mark added the emphasis on lack of faith to this story. As it stands, the text gives two contrasting explanations about why the disciples could not cast out the demon. At the conclusion, Jesus tells his students that what was needed was prayer. This sort of demon cannot be driven out "by anything except prayer." Earlier in the story, however, Jesus insists that the disciples' lack of faith is the problem. When the boy's father informs Jesus that his disciples have failed, Jesus responds, "O faithless generation!" Perhaps, then, Mark inserted material on the need for faith. Of course, in the edited story the two explanations do not actually contradict one another. Prayer strengthens faith.

As edited by Mark, this colorful narrative continues the pattern of declining miracles due to declining faith. In the previous miracle, Jesus had to lay his hands on the blind man twice to effect a total cure. However, at least the first attempt produced a positive result. The man went from total blindness to partial sight. By contrast, in the story we are presently considering, after Jesus orders the demon to come out, the boy goes into convulsions and almost dies. Only then is Jesus able to heal him by grasping the child's hand and raising him up. The story emphasizes that lack of faith is the problem. When the crowd initially sees Jesus, it is astonished. Similarly, when the father pleads with Jesus to help if he can, Jesus objects, "'If you can!' All things are possible to one who has faith!"

The story emphatically confirms another pattern in Mark: That Jesus tries to keep miracles secret if there is no faith, but works public miracles if there is. In response to Jesus' insistence that anything is possible with faith, the man shows that he has faith—but barely: "I believe; help my unbelief." Just as the man is on the border between faith and doubt, so the miracle is on the border between being private and public. Mark tells us that Jesus performed the exorcism "when Jesus saw that a crowd was running together." Interestingly, this detail contradicts the first part of the narrative and so must have been a clumsy addition which Mark made. The opening of the story tells us "a great crowd" was already present.

Within the larger structure of Mark, the details of this story suggest that the time for miracles has largely passed. In the preceeding chapters, the miracles have become more and more difficult as people's faith has become less and less. Now Jesus is barely able to work them. Meanwhile the cross looms larger and larger. Accordingly, Mark suggests that Jesus' mission to work miracles is basically over. Excluding the resurrection, there are only two more miracles in Mark, and, as we shall see, in both the symbolic meaning is more important than the wonder itself.

Questions for Reflection:

Do most of us come to Jesus in effect saying, "I believe; help my unbelief"? How does Jesus respond to this request today? What is the relationship between faith and prayer? In the Christian life do we sometimes get to a point when the time for miracles is basically over and we must now simply suffer? How can God be present in these times?

28.   Mark 9:30–37

And he went out from there and was passing by through Galilee, and he did not want anyone to know, for he was teaching his students and saying to them, "The son of humanity is given into the hands of human beings, and they will kill him, and when he has been killed, after three days he will rise." But they did not understand the saying, and they were afraid to ask him (9:30–32).

And they came to Capernaum. And when they were in the house, he asked them, "What were you discussing on the road?" But they were silent, for they had been discussing with one another on the road who was the greatest (9:33–34).

And after he sat down, he called the twelve and said to them, "If anyone wants to be first, they will be last of all and servant of all."

And he took a child and placed it in their midst, and when he had taken it into his arms, he said to them, "Whoever receives one such child in my name receives me, and whoever receives me, does not receive me, but him who sent me (9:35–37).

This block of material repeats both the themes and structure of the material associated with Jesus' first passion prediction. Once again, Jesus is trying to hide from the public to avoid acclaim and is teaching the disciples in private that he must suffer. However, once more, the disciples do not understand. Instead, they are arguing among themselves who is the greatest. In response, Jesus teaches the need for humble discipleship. Whoever would be first must be last.

Questions for Reflection:

> What does Jesus mean when he says that whoever receives even a child receives him? In what sense is it in fact true that the first is last and the last first? Is this true in the world? Is it true in the church? Is it true in heaven? Are those who are "last" able to have a deeper relationship with Jesus who made himself last by accepting the cross?

29.   Mark 9:38 – 10:31

John said to him, "Teacher, we saw someone driving out demons in your name, and we tried to stop him, because he was not following us." But Jesus said, "Do not stop him, for there is no one who will do a miracle in my name and will quickly be able to defame me, for whoever is not against us is for us. For whoever gives you a cup of water to drink in my name because you are Christians, truly I say to you that they will not lose their reward" (9:38–41).

"And whoever makes one of these little ones who believe fall, it would be better for them if instead a large millstone hung around their neck and they had been thrown into the sea. And if your hand makes you fall, cut it off. It is better for you to enter into life maimed than to have two hands and go away into Gehenna, to the inextinguishable fire. And if your foot makes you fall, cut it off. It is better for you to enter into life lame than to have two feet and be thrown into Gehenna. And if your eye makes you fall, throw it away. For you it is better with one eye to enter into God's rule than to have two eyes and be thrown into Gehenna, where their worm does not die, and the fire is not extinguished. For everyone will be salted with fire. Salt is good, but if the salt becomes tasteless, with what will you season it? Have salt among yourselves and live in peace with one another" (9:42–50).

And from there, he rose and came into the region of Judea across the Jordan, and again crowds were flocking to him. And, as he was accustomed, he again taught them. And the Pharisees came and asked him if it was allowed for a man to divorce his wife. They were testing him. And in reply he said to them, "What did Moses command you?" And they said, "Moses permitted writing a divorce certificate and sending her off." But Jesus said to them, "On account of your hardheadedness he wrote for you this commandment. But from the beginning of creation, 'He made them male and female.' 'Because of this a man will leave his father and mother . . . and the two will be one flesh.' So then, they are no longer two, but one flesh. Therefore, what God has yoked together, let no human being separate!" And back in the house the students asked him about this. And he said to them, "Whoever divorces his wife and marries another commits adultery against her. And if she divorces her husband and marries another, she commits adultery" (10:1–12).

And they were bringing children to him so he would touch them. But the disciples reprimanded them. But when Jesus saw it, he became indignant and said to them, "Let the children come to me; do not forbid them. For God's rule belongs to such as these. Truly I say to you, whoever does not receive God's rule as a child will not go into it at all." And taking them into his arms, he blessed them by laying his hands on them (10:13–16).

And as he was going out into the road, a man ran up and fell on his knees before him and asked him, "Good teacher, what am I to do so I may inherit eternal life?" But Jesus said to him, "Why do you call me good? No one is good except God only. You know the commandments: Do not murder, do not commit adultery, do not steal, do not testify falsely, do not defraud, honor your father and mother." And he said to him, "Teacher, all these things I have kept from my youth." And Jesus looking at him loved him and said to him, "One thing you lack: Go off, sell all you have and give to the poor, and you will have a treasure in heaven, and come, follow me!" But he was shocked at the saying and went away grieved, for he had much property (10:17–22).

And Jesus looked around and said to his students, "With what difficulty will those who have wealth go into God's rule!" But the students were amazed at his words. But Jesus, in reply, again said to them, "Children, how difficult it is to go into God's rule! It is easier for a camel to go through the eye of a needle than for a rich person to go into God's rule." But they were greatly astonished and said to one another, "And who can be saved?" Jesus looked at them and said, "With human beings it is impossible, but not with God! For all things are possible with God" (10:23–27).

Peter began to say to him, "Look, we left everything and have followed you." Jesus said, "Truly I say to you, there is no one who left a house or brothers or sisters or mother or father or children or lands on account of me and on account of the good news, who will not receive a hundred times as much now in this age, houses and brothers and sisters and mothers and children and lands, with persecutions, and in the coming age, eternal life. But many who are first will be last, and the last, first" (10:28–31).

There is no break between the second passion prediction and the material we are considering here. After the second passion prediction and the debate among the disciples about who is greatest, Jesus declares that the first must be last because whoever receives even a child in his name receives Jesus himself. The present section expands on this teaching and ends by reiterating that the "first will be last, and the last, first."

In this section, Mark passes on a series of teachings concerning how Christians should treat various people. The first block of material tells us that we must be charitable toward outsiders who are not hurting us. "Whoever is not against us is for us." Indeed, we may be confident that anyone who gives assistance to a Christian—even if it is no more than a "cup of water"—will certainly have a reward. The second block stresses that we must not cause anyone within the community to sin. Instead, we must live in peace with each other. The next blocks stress that we must not divorce our spouses and marry someone else and that we must always be open to the needs of children. Finally, we have a section warning the rich that they must give their possessions to the poor.

Mark then summarizes the message of the entire unit by stressing that Christians are to be a single family in which we are servants of one another. When Peter states, "We left everything and have followed you," he speaks for Mark's original Christian readers. They, too, gave up much to follow Jesus. In reply, Jesus insists that anyone who abandoned relatives or property will receive a hundred times as much even in this life. The way they will do so is evident. Every member of the church will be a brother or sister, parent or child to all other members, and everyone's property will be at the disposal of all. Hence, indeed "the first will be last, and the last, first."

By such solidarity, Mark's intended readers will be able to endure persecution. Evidently, at least many of Mark's readers had already lost their personal property and natural families. Moreover, as Mark emphasizes, when they followed Jesus and gained a hundred times as many relatives and a hundred times as much property, they also gained "persecutions." Apparently then, it is precisely by being a family, by supporting one another as brothers and sisters, that we will be able to endure the present tribulation and in the end gain "eternal life."

Mark's portrayal of the Christian family would naturally inspire Christians to resist church leaders who seek power and privilege during a period of crisis. In a time of catastrophe, church leaders may try to gain power and privilege for themselves by preying on people's fears and making extravagant promises, perhaps in the name of God. These leaders may claim that they are following the example of Jesus. Mark, however, insists that it is through solidarity with one another that Christians survive persecutions. Such solidarity thrives when those who would be first truly imitate Jesus and act as servants of all. Therefore, Mark's theology would encourage his readers not to follow Christian demagogues.

At the same time, however, Mark suggests we need not be overly critical of Christian prophets who are not part of the official leadership structure, as long as they are doing no harm. When John reports that he tried to censure an exorcist who was not obeying them (the twelve?), Jesus rebukes him. "Whoever is not against us is for us."

The story of the unauthorized exorcist also highlights the failure of the disciples who now seem to be spiritually inferior, even to outsiders. Previously, Jesus gave them the power to drive out demons (6:7), and they had successfully exorcised many people (6:13). However, by the time we get to chapter 9, the disciples apparently begin to lose this ability since they are unable to exorcise the epileptic boy. Now, Mark reports that an outsider is successfully casting out demons in Jesus' name.

Questions for Reflection:

In what ways are Christians today a single family? In what ways are we not? Is it true in our experience that "whoever is not against us is for us"? Do Christian individuals or

groups who are not part of "official" Christianity sometimes accomplish things that members of the church cannot
do? How do we respond to such individuals and groups?

30.   Mark 10:32–45

*Now they were going up on the road to Jerusalem, and Jesus was
going ahead of them, and they were amazed, and those who
followed were afraid. And he again took aside the twelve and began
to tell them the things that were about to happen to him. "Look,
we are going up to Jerusalem, and the son of humanity will be
handed over to the chief priests and to the scribes, and they will
condemn him to death, and they will hand him over to the
Gentiles, and they will ridicule him and spit on him and whip him
and kill him, and after three days he will rise" (10:32–34).*

*And James and John, Zebedee's sons, came to him and said to
him, "Teacher, we want you to do for us whatever we ask you."
And he said to them, "What do you want me to do for you?" And
they said to him, "Grant to us that we may sit, one at your right
and one at your left, in your glory." But Jesus said to them, "You
do not know what you are asking. Can you drink the cup which I
drink or be baptized with the baptism with which I am baptized?"
But they said to him, "We can." But Jesus said to them, "The cup
which I drink you will drink, and with the baptism with which I
am baptized you will be baptized. But to sit on my right or on my
left is not mine to give, but it is for those for whom it has been
prepared." And when the ten heard, they began to be angry at
James and John. And Jesus summoned them and said to them,
"You know that those who are recognized to rule over the Gentiles
lord it over them, and their great tyrannize them. But it is not this
way among you, but whoever wants to become great among you
will be your servant, and whoever wants to be first among you will*

be slave of all. For the son of humanity also did not come to be served, but to serve and to give his life as a ransom for many" (10:35–45).

The third passion prediction basically resembles the others and brings the section which begins with Peter's confession to a close. Throughout the section Jesus has been steadily leading his disciples toward Jerusalem. Now, he explicitly points out to them (and the reader) that their destination is near. Once again, Jesus foretells his suffering and death, though this time he does so in much greater detail. Then again, we have a negative reaction from the disciples. James and John ask to sit at Jesus' right and left in the kingdom, and when the ten hear, they are angry. Finally, we have the teaching about the need for humble servanthood. Those who would be great must be servants of all in imitation of Jesus who is giving his life as a ransom for others.

As in the previous passion predictions, we get no hint that the disciples understand, and their lack of understanding challenges the reader to do better. The beginning of the story especially stresses the disciples' obtuseness. As Jesus leads them toward Jerusalem, they are "amazed." The reader, however, should remember the first two passion predictions and not be surprised. Jesus is humble and must suffer, and we must be humble and suffer too.

Questions for Reflection:

Are we able to drink Jesus' cup of suffering? How can we become more able? Are members of the church today—and, especially, members of the leadership—often more concerned with getting the places of honor than with imitating Jesus?

31.   Mark 10:46–52

And they came to Jericho. And as he and his students and a considerable crowd were going out of Jericho, the son of Timaeus, Bartimaeus, a blind beggar, was sitting beside the road. And when he heard that it was Jesus of Nazareth, he began to shout, "Son of David, Jesus, have mercy on me!" And many reprimanded him so he would be quiet. But he shouted much louder, "Son of David, have mercy on me!" And Jesus stopped and said, "Call him." And they called the blind man by saying to him, "Cheer up, rise, he is calling you." And he threw off his coat and jumped to his feet and came to Jesus. And in response to him, Jesus said, "What do you want me to do for you?" And the blind man said to him, "My Master, let me see again!" And Jesus said to him, "Go, your faith has saved you." And at once he could see again, and he followed him on the road (10:46–52).

We may suspect that Mark altered the traditional end of this story by adding that Bartimaeus followed him *"on the road."* In the oral tradition, this detail would probably not have been remembered. Indeed, the detail would be pointless if the story were told separately. We would not even know what the road in question was. Moreover, in the story as Mark tells it, the detail is disturbing. After all, Jesus tells Bartimaeus to go, but instead of going, Bartimaeus follows him. Strikingly, even though Matthew and Luke both take the story from Mark, neither retains this odd concluding phrase.

The healing of Bartimaeus is a transitional narrative which links the passion predictions with the passion itself. As we have seen, just before this miracle Jesus gives the last and most detailed passion prediction. Immediately after it, Jesus approaches Jerusalem where the passion will take place.

Within Mark's overall structure, the story balances the healing of the blind man at Bethsaida and consequently also symbolizes that true sight is accepting the cross. The first healing of a blind man comes immediately before the first passion prediction. The second comes immediately after the last. Since, as we have seen, the first miracle symbolizes what partial and full sight are, we might expect that some similar symbolism may be present in this second story. In fact, the story suggests that true sight is to follow Jesus on the way to the cross. As soon as Bartimaeus is healed, we read "he followed him on the road." The phrase "on the road" occurs in each of the three units predicting the passion (8:27, 9:33, 10:32). Accordingly, the "road" is the road to the crucifixion.

The miracle fits well with the pattern that Jesus willingly works public miracles if there is faith. Bartimaeus shows his belief in Jesus by his persistence and eagerness in trying to reach him. When he hears that Jesus has come, he shouts for Jesus to have mercy on him, and when the crowd tries to hush him, he shouts louder. When he learns that Jesus has summoned him, he throws off his coat and jumps to his feet. After Jesus heals him, Jesus himself declares that it is Bartimaeus's *faith* which has saved him. Because there is faith, Mark emphasizes that the miracle is fully public. Not only are the disciples present, but there is also "a considerable crowd."

The story demonstrates that it is the previous lack of faith which has been reducing Jesus' ability to perform miracles. After the continuing decline in Jesus' power to work wonders (see above), the effortlessness with which he heals Bartimaeus is striking. Jesus does not have to try twice or use saliva or lay his hands on the sufferer. Strictly speaking, he does not even pronounce a healing word (cf., e.g., "be opened"; 7:34). If there is faith, miracles are easy, indeed so easy that Jesus can declare that it is Bartimaeus's faith that has saved him.

The story reverses Jesus' previous pattern of trying to keep the public from realizing that he is the Messiah, God's Son. As we have seen, previously Jesus always tries to silence anyone, whether a demon or a human being, who proclaims who Jesus really is. Now, we have the opposite. The crowd tries to silence

Bartimaeus when he addresses Jesus as "Son of David," and
Jesus himself insists that Bartimaeus come forward.

The reason the story reverses the pattern is that Jesus is on
the verge of being crucified, and so secrecy is no longer needed.
Up to this time, Jesus has attempted to hide his true identity so
that people would not keep him from going to Jerusalem and
being crucified. Immediately after the healing of Bartimaeus,
Jesus arrives in the environs of Jerusalem. Now there is no
longer any danger that he will escape death. Indeed, as we shall
see, it is precisely by insisting publicly that he is the Messiah,
God's Son, that Jesus will force his enemies to kill him.

Questions for Reflection:

Today does the proclamation that Jesus is God's Son comfort the world or fundamentally attack its assumptions and
values? Will someone who truly represents "Christian values" have an easier or harder time getting elected to public
office or rising in a corporation? Is it faith that heals or is
it God? How does Christian faith work differently than
such things as "positive thinking" and "self-actualization"?

32.   Mark 11:1–25

*And when they got near to Jerusalem to Bethphage and Bethany
toward the Mount of Olives, he sent out two of his students by
saying to them, "Go off into the village opposite you, and as you
go into it, at once you will find a tethered colt on which no person
has yet sat. Untie it and bring it. And if anyone says to you, 'Why
are you doing this?' say, 'The Lord has need of it, and at once he
is going to send it back here.'" And they went away and found the
colt tethered by a door outside on the street, and they untied it. And*

some of those standing there said to them, "What are you doing, untieing the colt?" And they told them just what Jesus said, and they let them take it. And they brought the colt to Jesus, and they put their coats on it, and he sat on it. And many spread their coats on the road, and others cut down leafy branches from the fields. And those who went before and those who followed kept shouting, "Hosanna! Blessed is he who is coming in the Lord's name. Blessed is the coming rule of our father David! Hosanna in the highest!" And he went into Jerusalem into the temple, and he looked around at everything, and since the hour was late already, he went out to Bethany with the twelve (11:1–11).

And on the next day, as they were coming out from Bethany, he became hungry. And when from a distance he saw a fig tree with leaves on it, he came to it to see if perhaps he would find something on it. And when he came to it, he found nothing except leaves, for it was not the season for figs. And in response he said to it, "From now on, may no one eat fruit from you forever!" And his students heard (11:12–14).

And they came into Jerusalem. And after he came into the temple, he began to drive out those who sold and bought in the temple, and he overturned the tables of the moneychangers and the seats of those who sold the doves. And he did not let anyone carry a vessel through the temple. And in his teaching he said to them, "Isn't it written, 'My house will be called a house of prayer for all the nations'? But you have made it a bandits' den!" And the chief priests and the scribes heard it, and they sought how they might kill him, for they were afraid of him, for all the crowd was astonished over his teaching. And when it became late, he went out of the city (11:15–19).

And as they were going by early in the morning, they saw the fig tree withered from the roots. And Peter was reminded and said to him, "Rabbi, see, the fig tree which you cursed has withered." And in reply Jesus said to them, "Have faith in God. Truly I say to you that whoever says to this mountain, 'Be lifted up and thrown into the sea!' and does not waver in their heart but believes that what they say will take place, they will have it. For this reason I tell you, believe that everything you pray and ask for that you have received it, and it will be yours. And when you stand praying, forgive if you are holding anything against anyone, so your Father in heaven will also forgive you your trespasses" (11:20–25).

We must suppose that, in the oral tradition, Jesus' triumphant entry into Jerusalem, his protest in the temple courts, and the cursing of the fig tree were all independent stories. People would have had difficulty remembering connections between them and surely would have told them separately, at least on occasion. It is striking that John's gospel does tell the cleansing of the temple separately and, indeed, places it at an earlier point in Jesus' ministry (John 2:13–22).

Mark however, carefully weaves these stories together. At the conclusion of the triumphant entry, Jesus goes into the temple courts and looks around but does nothing further because "the hour was late already." Instead, he goes to Bethany. As he is returning to the temple the next day, he curses a fig tree, but apparently nothing happens to the tree immediately. Jesus next stages a protest in the temple and again withdraws from Jerusalem. The following morning, he and his disciples pass the fig tree which now is completely withered.

Because of this interweaving, the fig tree and its fate symbolize the temple. By placing the cleansing of the temple between the cursing of the fig tree and its actual destruction, Mark invites the reader to compare the tree and the sacred place. Just as the fig tree has leaves but no fruit, so the temple is outwardly beautiful but spiritually barren. Just as the fig tree is destroyed after a short interval, so too in a short time the temple will be destroyed. Later, we will see that this destruction occurred about the time Mark was writing and thus had a special significance for his intended readers.

The cursing of the fig tree also brings to a climax the series of decreasing miracles due to decreasing faith. Earlier, we saw how two previous miracles, the healing of the blind man at Bethsaida (8:22–26) and the healing of the epileptic boy

(9:14–29) required a little time to take effect. Now, with the fig tree, the miracle apparently does not occur for an entire day. Then, when Peter sees that the tree has withered, he seems to be surprised. In response, Jesus exhorts the disciples to have faith and assures them that if only they do not doubt, they will even be able to move mountains. The implication is clear. The disciples' lack of faith made the fig tree wither so slowly.

Jesus is free to encourage the crowd to acclaim him because at this point, that very acclamation will lead to his death. Now that he has arrived in the vicinity of Jerusalem, Jesus sets in motion the events that will necessitate his rejection and execution. Thus, Jesus orchestrates the triumphant entry. He sends the disciples to get the colt and rides into the city. The crowd responds by proclaiming that he is the one who comes in the Lord's name, and in this context, the acclamation suggests clearly that he is the Messiah. Indeed, the crowd exclaims: "Blessed is the coming rule of our father David." Next, Jesus stages a dramatic—even violent—protest in the temple. The combination of the triumphant entry and the temple demonstration inflames popular enthusiasm, and this acclaim in turn forces the authorities to plot to kill Jesus. Mark explicitly states, "They sought how they might kill him, for they were afraid of him, for all the crowd was astonished over his teaching." Significantly, this sentence was probably added by Mark, since the story of the cleansing of the temple is complete without it.

Questions for Reflection:

Is the church today sometimes outwardly beautiful and successful but spiritually barren? If so, what leads to this paradox? If a church is spiritually barren, will it ultimately be destroyed if it does not repent? Is it true today that no matter what we ask for in prayer we will receive it if we believe?

⇥ ❋ ⇤

33.   Mark 11:27 - 12:37

And they came back into Jerusalem. And as he was walking about in the temple, the chief priests and the scribes and the elders came to him, and they said to him, "By what authority are you doing these things? Or who gave you this authority to do them?" And Jesus said to them, "I will ask you one thing, and you answer me. Then I will tell you by what authority I am doing these things. Was John's baptism from heaven or from human beings? Answer me." And they discussed it with one another saying, "What are we to say? If we say, 'From heaven,' he will say, 'so why did you not believe him?' but are we to say, 'From human beings'?" They were afraid of the crowd, for all held that John actually was a prophet. And in reply to Jesus they said, "We do not know." And Jesus said to them, "Nor am I going to tell you by what authority I am doing these things" (11:27–33).

And he began to speak to them in parables, "A person planted a vineyard and put a wall around it and dug a pit for the wine press and built a tower and leased it to tenant farmers and went off on a journey. At the proper time, he sent out a slave to the tenants to receive from the tenants some of the vineyard's fruit. And they took him and beat him and sent him out empty-handed. And again he sent out another slave to them. And that one they hit on the head and insulted. And he sent out another, and that one they killed. And many others, some they beat, and some they killed. He had still one more person, a beloved son. He sent him out last to them, saying, 'They will be shamed by my son.' But those tenants said to each other, 'This is the heir! Come, let us kill him, and the inheritance will be ours!' And they seized and killed him and threw him out of the vineyard. So what will the owner of the vineyard do? He will come and destroy the tenants and will give the vineyard to others. And haven't you read this scripture, 'A stone that the builders rejected, this has become the cornerstone. This is from the

Lord, and in our eyes it is wonderful'?" And they wished to arrest him, but they were afraid of the crowd, for they knew that he had spoken the parable against them. And they left him and went away (12:1–12).

And they sent out to him some of the Pharisees and the Herodians to catch him in his talk. And they came and said to him, "Teacher, we know that you are true, and court no one's favor, for you do not show partiality, but you teach truly the way of God. Is it allowed to give poll tax to Caesar or not? Shall we give it or shall we not?" But knowing their hypocrisy, he said to them, "Why are you testing me? Bring me a denarius so I may see it." And they brought one. And he said to them, "Whose is this image and inscription?" And they said to him, "Caesar's." And Jesus said to them, "Give Caesar's things back to Caesar, and God's to God." And they were astounded at him (12:13–17).

And the Sadducees, who say there is no resurrection, came to him, and they asked him, "Teacher, Moses wrote for us that if someone's brother dies and leaves behind a wife and does not leave a child, his brother is to take the wife and raise up an offspring for his brother. There were seven brothers. And the first took a wife and, when he died, did not leave an offspring. And the second took her and died and did not leave behind an offspring. And the third likewise. And the seven did not leave an offspring. Last of all, the woman also died. In the resurrection, when they rise, whose wife will she be? For the seven had her as a wife." Jesus said to them, "Is it not for this reason that you are mistaken, that you know neither the Scriptures nor God's power? For when they rise from the dead, they neither marry nor are given in marriage, but are like angels in heaven. But concerning the dead that they are raised, have you not read in the book of Moses, in the passage about the bush, how God said to him, 'I am Abraham's God, and Isaac's God, and Jacob's God'? He is not God of the dead but of the living. You are much mistaken" (12:18–27).

And one of the scribes who had heard them debating and saw that he answered them well came to him and asked him, "Which commandment is first of all?" Jesus answered, "The first is, 'Listen,

Israel, the Lord our God is the one Lord, and you shall love the Lord your God with your whole heart and your whole soul and your whole mind and your whole strength.' The second is this, 'You shall love your neighbor as yourself.' No other commandment is greater than these." And the scribe said to him, "Well spoken, teacher! You have said the truth that he is the only one, and there is no other than he, and to love him with the whole heart and with the whole understanding and with the whole strength and to love one's neighbor as oneself is much greater than all whole burnt offerings and sacrifices." And when Jesus saw that he answered thoughtfully, he said to him, "You are not far from God's rule." And no one any longer dared to question him (12:28–34).

And in response, Jesus said, as he was teaching in the temple, "How can the scribes say that the Messiah is David's Son? David himself said by the Holy Spirit, 'The Lord said to my Lord, "Sit at my right until I put your enemies underneath your feet."' David himself calls him 'Lord.' So how is he his son?" And the great crowd heard him gladly (12:35–37).

In this section, Mark has grouped together a number of originally independent stories in which Jesus spars with various Jewish authorities. Thus, we have a confrontation between Jesus and the chief priests, scribes, and elders over the source of his authority. Then, Jesus tells a parable in which he foretells that they will kill him and ultimately be destroyed themselves. After that, he evades a trap set by the Pharisees and Herodians concerning paying taxes to Caesar. Next, he replies to the Sadducees who try to show that resurrection is impossible. A more friendly dialogue follows between Jesus and a scribe about which commandment is central. Finally, Jesus himself asks his hearers to judge whether the scribes are correct when they claim that the Messiah is David's son.

Of course, these stories taken individually contain some of the most important teaching in Mark. For example, as Jesus insists, loving God and loving your neighbor are crucial.

Scarcely less important is faith in the resurrection, which Jesus eloquently defends against the sophistry of the Sadducees.

Within the structure of the gospel as a whole, however, what is especially significant about these stories is that in them Jesus publicly suggests that he is God's Son, and he does so in order to provoke opposition. Thus, both the opening and the closing of the section hint strongly that Jesus is God's Son. The section opens with Jesus suggesting that his authority comes from the same source as John's baptism, and that can only mean directly from God. The following parable about the vineyard owner and the tenants is a transparent allegory in which the owner of the vineyard is God and his Son is none other than Jesus himself. Moreover, in case Jesus' hearers—or Mark's readers—somehow miss the point, Mark then adds a scriptural citation about a rejected stone becoming the cornerstone. The stone in question is Jesus. Jesus, therefore, is God's Son, and God will exalt him as the "cornerstone" of the coming kingdom. The closing unit in the series also generously hints that Jesus is more than a mere human being. By showing that the Messiah is David's Lord, Jesus clearly implies that the Messiah is not David's son, but God's. Of course, such claims help provoke opposition. At the end of the parable about the vineyard we read, "They wished to arrest him . . . for they knew that he had spoken the parable against them." In the closing story, Jesus is attacking the scribes directly, since it is they who erroneously teach that the Messiah is merely David's son.

Because Jesus is fanning opposition which will lead to his death, Mark emphasizes that he is no longer trying to avoid public acclaim. On the contrary, Mark concludes the series of confrontations between the authorities and Jesus with the striking sentence, "The great crowd heard him gladly."

Questions for Reflection:

If we loved God and Jesus above all else, would we be more popular today or less? To love God above all else, must we believe that "the Lord our God is the one Lord"? If there is one God and Jesus is his only Son, what belongs to Caesar?

34.   Mark 12:38–44

And in his teaching he said, "Watch out for the scribes who like to walk around in long robes and greetings in the marketplaces and the best seats in the synagogues and the places of honor at banquets, who eat up widows' houses and for appearance pray at length. These will receive severe condemnation" (12:38–40).

And he sat opposite the treasury and watched how the crowd was throwing money into the treasury. And many rich people were throwing in much. And one poor widow came and threw in two copper coins which equal a quadrant. And he summoned his students and said to them, "Truly I tell you that this poor widow threw in more than all who were throwing into the treasury. For they were throwing in from their abundance, but this woman from her scarcity threw in all that she had, her whole living" (12:41–44).

Mark ends the confrontation between Jesus and his enemies by reminding the reader that Jesus rejects religious leaders who seek their own comfort and praises all who are self-sacrificing. Jesus concludes his attack on the scribes by emphasizing that they seek social prestige and exploit the helpless. He contrasts this self-seeking with the generosity of a poor widow who gives away all that she has. Significantly, Mark tells us that Jesus held up the widow as an example to his *students.*

Mark is making the same point here to the reader that he made with the passion predictions. Christians—especially, Christian leaders—who seek their own good will come to eternal ruin, whereas those who deny themselves will imitate Jesus and receive his praise. It is also significant that in the next section, Mark will directly attack Christian leaders of his own time.

Questions for Reflection:

> Do Christians today sometimes pray only for appearance's sake? What are the marks of genuine prayer? Do the poor contribute more than the rich?

35.   Mark 13:1–37

And as he was going out of the temple, one of his students said to him, "Teacher, look what stones and what buildings!" And Jesus said to him, "You see these great buildings? There will not be left here a stone on top of a stone that will not be thrown down" (13:1–2).

And as he was sitting on the Mount of Olives opposite the temple, Peter and James and John and Andrew asked him privately, "Tell us when these things will be and what will be the sign when all these things are about to be accomplished" (13:3–4).

And Jesus began to say to them, "Watch out, lest anyone mislead you. Many will come in my name saying, 'I am he,' and they will mislead many (13:5–6).

"But when you hear of wars and rumors of wars, do not be alarmed. It must happen, but the end is not yet. For nation will rise up against nation and kingdom against kingdom. There will be earthquakes in various places; there will be famines. These things

are the beginning of the labor pains. As for you, watch out your-selves! They will hand you over to the councils, and you will be beaten in the synagogues, and you will be made to stand before governors and kings on account of me for testimony to them. And the good news must first be proclaimed to all the nations. And when they bring you to hand you over, do not worry beforehand what you are to say. But whatever is given to you at that hour, say this. For you are not the ones speaking, but the Holy Spirit. And brother will hand over brother to death, and father will hand over his child, and children will rise up against parents and have them put to death. And you will be hated by all because of my name. But those who endure to the end will be saved (13:7–13).

"But when you see the devastating sacrilege standing where it must not be" (let the reader take note!), "then let those in Judea flee to the mountains; let those upon the roof not come down nor go in to take anything from their house; and let those in the field not turn back to take their coat. And alas for those who are pregnant and those who nurse in those days. And pray that it may not happen in winter. For those days will be an affliction such as has not hap-pened from the beginning of creation (which God created) until now and will not happen. And if the Lord had not shortened the days, no flesh would be saved. But because of the chosen whom he chose, he shortened the days. And then if anyone says to you, 'Look here! It is the Messiah!' 'Look there!' Do not believe it. For false messiahs and false prophets will rise up and will give signs and wonders to lead astray, if possible, the chosen. Now you watch out. I have told you everything beforehand! (13:14–23).

"But in those days, after that affliction, the sun will be darkened, and the moon will not give her radiance, and the stars will be falling from heaven, and the powers in the heavens will be shaken. And then they will see the son of humanity coming in the clouds with great power and glory. And then he will send out the angels and gather together the chosen from the four winds, from the end of the earth until the end of heaven (13:24–27).

"From the fig tree learn a metaphor. When its branch has already become soft and put out leaves, you know that summer is near.

So, you too, when you see these things happening, realize that he is near, at your doors. Truly I say to you that this generation will not pass away until all these things happen. Heaven and earth will pass away, but my words will not pass away. But about that day or hour no one knows, not even the angels in heaven, nor the Son, only the Father. Be alert, keep awake, for you do not know when the time is. It is like a person away on a trip who left their house and gave responsibility to their slaves, a job for each, and commanded the doorkeeper to watch. So, watch! For you do not know when the master of the house is coming, whether in the evening or at midnight or cockcrow or in the morning, lest coming unexpectedly, he finds you sleeping. And what I say to you, I say to all, watch!" (13:28–37).

U p to this point, Mark's gospel has dealt with the past and must have seemed uncontroversial to its first Christian readers. So far, the evangelist has avoided making direct comments about contemporary church affairs. Instead, he has passed on what presumably were familiar and beloved stories. The narrative as a whole resembles an ancient biography, and so readers could have assumed they were basically experiencing a "life of Jesus." To be sure, Mark has shaped the material in a personal way. However, at this time the traditions about Jesus mostly lacked fixed wording or order, and every Christian who passed on the material had to shape it.

In this section, however, Mark gives us a sketch of church history virtually from the time of Jesus to the end of the world. According to the outline, during the first period of church history there will be various catastrophes in the larger world, including wars, earthquakes, and famines. Meanwhile, Christians will preach the good news throughout the world and suffer persecution and public hatred. Accordingly, patient endurance will be essential. Next, there will be a supreme crisis. The suffering will be more extreme than in all of previous human history. As a result, Christians will face an unparalleled temptation to fall away. Indeed, if God had not shortened this terrible time, no one would be able to remain faithful. During this dire period, false prophets and false messiahs will appear and work miracles in an effort to mislead Christians. Finally, the world will end. The heavenly bodies will collapse, and Jesus will return and save his chosen.

In providing this sketch, Mark has drastically shaped earlier traditions. Much—perhaps most—of the basic material Mark took from the oral tradition, and presumably the majority goes back to Jesus himself. Nevertheless, Mark has carefully molded it. Indeed, he has not hesitated to intervene so dramatically that at least a few sections clash with their settings. It is startling to read in the midst of a speech by Jesus, "Let the reader take note!" Scarcely less disturbing is the conclusion in which Jesus supposedly says in private to Peter, James, John, and Andrew, "And what I say to you, I say to all, watch!"

From Mark's careful editing of the section, we can see that he is writing during the period of supreme crisis. Of course, Mark's intrusive comment, "Let the reader take note!" makes it especially obvious that his principal concern is the horrifying events he now relates. Nevertheless, there are other editorial indications. For example, it is interesting that Jesus begins his private comments to Peter, James, John, and Andrew by warning that people will come in his name and try to lead others astray. In the subsequent outline of church history, we read no more about these false prophets until the period of supreme crisis. Hence, Jesus' opening comment is not about the first thing that will happen, but rather is a summary of the most important point Mark is making for the reader.

Mark clearly implies that one of the events that will take place during this dreadful period is the destruction of the temple, and so we may assume that he is writing around the year 70 BCE and is responding to Nero's persecution and the Jewish War. The section begins with an unnamed disciple remarking on the glories of the temple and Jesus' solemn prediction that the structure will be utterly ruined. Jesus' actual speech is a response to a request that he specify "when these things will be." Therefore, it seems clear that Mark is writing about the time of the temple's destruction. Since the Roman armies destroyed the building in 70 BCE, we must assume that the events in church history which occurred around that year were especially relevant to Mark and his audience. The two most important were Nero's persecution of Christians in Rome, which occurred from around 65 CE until 68 CE, and the war between the Jews and Rome, which lasted from 66 CE until 70 CE.

As Mark suggests, this period was catastrophic for the church. After the great fire of Rome in 64 CE, there were rumors that Nero himself had arranged for the conflagration so that he could rebuild the capital on a grander scale. Accordingly, he needed a scapegoat and fastened on the Roman Christians. He accused them of arson and began executing them, often in horrifying and grotesque ways, including burning them alive. Then in 66 CE, the Jews in Palestine revolted, and for the next four years, Palestine was decimated by battles between Jewish and Roman forces. Presumably, both sides persecuted Christians. The Romans would have regarded them as Jews, whereas the rebels would have regarded any sect which was open to Gentile membership as collaborators.

Mark makes it clear that his principal concern is to keep his readers from trying to escape suffering by following the false messiahs. Throughout Jesus' description of coming events, we get various warnings that the suffering will be intense and endurance necessary. Thus, these themes already appear in the description of the first period of church history—even though this era was past for Mark and his readers. Mark stresses that Christians will suffer death and universal odium and ends the section by reminding us, "But those who endure to the end will be saved." Of course, "the end" includes the period of catastrophe that Mark then describes. The warnings become more shrill as Mark narrates this time of crisis. He insists the sufferings will be so intense that endurance will be practically impossible. Indeed, if God had not shortened the time, no one could be

saved. Accordingly, we must especially beware. Finally, Jesus'
discourse ends with repeated warnings to "watch!" What we are
to beware of is the seduction of the false prophets and messiahs.
As we noted above, Jesus begins his private comments by
warning us against people who will come in his name. Then he
emphatically repeats these warnings as he describes their ad-
vent during the time of catastrophe. From the perspective of
the Christian readers for whom Mark was writing, it is especially
significant that Jesus warns that these false prophets would
"lead astray, if possible, the chosen," since that includes the
readers. Significantly, Mark ends the discourse by addressing
the readers once again and warning us that we must remain
steadfast: "What I say to you, I say to all, watch!"

From what Mark tells us, it appears that the false prophets
and messiahs were attractive for two reasons. First, they were
Christians and claimed to be faithful to the example of Jesus.
In the discourse, Jesus warns the Christian reader that these
imposters will come in his own name. Second, they worked
miracles. Jesus warns they "will give signs and wonders to lead
astray, if possible, the chosen."

Consequently, Mark implicitly invites his intended readers
to compare the message and the miracles of the false messiahs
with those of Jesus. The false messiahs claim to be faithful to
the example of Jesus. Yet this claim, at least according to Mark,
is a lie. Therefore, in reality, their message and their miracles
differ radically from those of Jesus. In his book, Mark presents
Jesus' message and miracles and, by implication, invites us to
contrast them with those of the Christian prophets who have
arisen lately. In this gospel Jesus emphasizes that he and his
followers must be "servants of all" (9:35) and "take up their
cross" (8:34). He also never works miracles to escape suffering
or inspire faith or gain public approval. Presumably, the "false
messiahs" whose "signs and wonders" might mislead the chosen
had a different approach.

Mark also tells his readers that soon they will see the real Messiah, who will reward those who have been faithful. After the brief period of tribulation "they will see the son of humanity," and he will gather his elect.

Now Mark will go on to narrate the most moving part of Jesus' life: His suffering and death and forcefully remind readers what kind of Messiah Jesus was.

Questions for Reflection:

Are there Christian miracle workers today who use signs and wonders to promote their own glory and deceive people concerning what following Jesus means? Would Mark's message have been different if he had not been writing during a period of persecution? How are Mark's warnings relevant to us who do not live in a time and place where the church is suffering catastrophically? Was Mark mistaken when he proclaimed that Jesus would return relatively soon? Should we today assume that Jesus will return during our lifetime, or instead, that we will meet Jesus when we die?

36.   Mark 14:1–11

Now the Passover and the holiday of unleavened bread were two days away. And the chief priests and the scribes were seeking how to seize him by deceit and kill him, for they were saying, "Not on the festival, lest there be a disturbance among the people" (14:1–2).

And while he was in Bethany in the house of Simon the leper, when he was dining, a woman came who had an alabaster jar of perfume, spikenard in pistachio oil, very expensive. She broke the jar and poured the perfume down on his head. Now there were some people who became indignant among themselves, "Why did this waste of perfume happen? For this perfume could have been sold for over three hundred days' wages and the proceeds been given to the poor!" And they scolded her. But Jesus said, "Let her be! Why are you bothering her? She has indeed done a beautiful deed to me. For you always have the poor with yourselves, and whenever you want, you can do a kindness to them, but you are not always going to have me. She did what she could. She perfumed my body in advance for burial. Truly I say to you, wherever the good news is proclaimed in the whole world, what she did will also be told as her memorial" (14:3–9).

And Judas Iscariot, one of the twelve, went away to the chief priests to betray him to them. And when they heard, they were glad and promised to give him money. And he was seeking a good time to betray him (14:10–11).

The beginning and end of this unit tell how the plot against Jesus is developing. Thus, at the start of the section, the chief priests and scribes want to seize Jesus, but they hesitate to do so lest there be a riot. At the end of the section, Judas offers to hand him over to them and so solves their problem.

By inserting the story of the woman pouring perfume on Jesus within the narration of the betrayal, Mark invites us to compare the woman's action with that of Judas. Originally, the story of the perfume was probably independent of the story of the betrayal. When people repeated these two narratives orally, it would have been difficult to combine them in the way they appear in Mark. Hence, Mark produced the sandwich arrangement himself. Literarily, sandwiching these stories invites the reader to look at them together and compare.

Viewed together, the stories contrast the faithfulness of the anonymous woman with the perfidy of one of Jesus' leading students. In the story, Mark stresses that the woman is otherwise unknown. He simply introduces her as a person who came and poured perfume over Jesus. At the end of the narrative, we read that it is this deed alone which will be her memorial. By contrast, Mark explicitly reminds us that Judas is "one of the twelve." Of course, the woman's actions are praiseworthy, whereas Judas's are evil.

Perhaps Mark intends for his readers to view Judas's actions as a warning against the false prophets and false messiahs. Just a few verses earlier Mark has emphasized that Christian leaders will try to mislead the chosen and that the reader must beware. Now in the narrative, Mark gives us an example of a Christian leader who betrays Jesus.

Questions for Reflection:

Are the official leaders of the church usually more or less faithful to Jesus than the ordinary members? What are the special gifts that leaders have? What are the special dangers that come with leadership?

37. Mark 14:12–52

And on the first day of unleavened bread, when they were slaughtering the Passover lamb, his students said to him, "Where do you want us to go and prepare so you may eat the Passover?" And he sent out two of his students by saying to them, "Go off into the city, and a person carrying a water jar will meet you. Follow him, and wherever he enters, say to the master of the house, 'The teacher says, "Where is my dining room where I may eat the Passover with my students?"' And he will show you a big upstairs room furnished and prepared. And there prepare for us." And the students went out and came into the city and found it just as he said to them, and they prepared the Passover (14:12–16).

And when it was evening, he came with the twelve. And as they were reclining and eating, Jesus said, "Truly I say to you that one of you will betray me, one eating with me." They began to be distressed and to say to him, one by one, "I am not the one, surely not I?" And he said to them, "One of the twelve who is dipping with me into the bowl, because the son of humanity is departing, just as it is written about him, but alas for that person through whom the son of humanity is betrayed. Better for him if that person had not been born!" (14:17–21).

And while they were eating, he took bread, said a blessing, broke the bread, and gave it to them and said, "Take it, this is my body." And he took a cup, gave thanks, and gave it to them, and all drank from it. And he said to them, "This is my blood of the covenant poured out for many. Truly I say to you that I will never drink from the produce of the vine again until that day when I drink it new in God's rule." And they sang a hymn and went out to the Mount of Olives (14:22–26).

And Jesus said to them, "All of you will fall away, because it is written, 'I will strike down the shepherd, and the sheep will be scattered.' But after I am raised, I will go before you into Galilee." But Peter said to him, "Even if all fall away, nevertheless I will not." And Jesus said to him, "Truly I say to you that on this very night before the cock twice crows, you will disown me three times." But he kept saying emphatically, "If I must die with you, I will not disown you." And all of them also said the same (14:27–31).

And they came to a place whose name is Gethsemane, and he said to his students, "Sit here while I pray." And he took along Peter and James and John with him, and he began to be appalled and distracted, and he said to them, "My heart is mortally wounded with grief. Stay here and watch." And he went ahead a little and fell on the ground and prayed that if it were possible the hour would pass by him, and he said, "Abba" (Father), "all things are possible for you. Take this cup away from me. Nevertheless, not what I want, but what you want." And he came and found them sleeping, and he said to Peter, "Simon, you are sleeping! You could have watched for one hour, couldn't you? Watch and pray that you do

*not come into temptation. The spirit is eager, but the flesh, weak."
And he went away again and prayed, saying the same words. And
he came back and found them sleeping, for their eyes were heavy,
and they did not know what to answer him. And he came a third
time and said to them, "You are sleeping still and resting up! The
matter is settled; the hour has come. Look, the son of humanity is
being betrayed into the hands of sinners. Get up, let us go. Look,
the man who is betraying me has gotten near" (14:32–42).*

*And at once, while he was still speaking, Judas, one of the twelve,
arrived and with him a crowd with swords and clubs from the chief
priests and the scribes and the elders. Now the man who was
betraying him had given them a signal saying, "Whomever I kiss,
he is the one. Seize him and lead him off securely." And he came
at once and approached him and said, "Rabbi," and he kissed him
devotedly. And they grabbed him with their hands and arrested
him. And one of the bystanders drew a sword and struck the high
priest's slave and cut off his earlobe. And in response, Jesus said
to them, "Have you come out with swords and clubs to arrest me
as if I were a bandit? I was with you teaching daily in the temple,
and you did not seize me. But it is so the Scriptures may be
fulfilled." And they all abandoned him and fled. And a certain
young man was also following with him, wearing a piece of linen
over his naked body, and they grabbed him. But he left behind the
linen and fled naked (14:43–52).*

Mark stresses that Judas is part of Jesus' intimate community and yet betrays him utterly. Mark states repeatedly
that Judas is "one of the twelve." Judas eats with Jesus—indeed,
shares the eucharist with him! Then Judas betrays him while
calling him "Rabbi," and kissing "him devotedly."

Perhaps Mark intends his narrative to be a solemn warning
to any Christian reader who might be considering becoming one
of the "false messiahs." Certainly, the scene in which each of
the twelve solemnly asks himself whether he is the one who will
betray Jesus is both dramatic and moving. Maybe then, Mark
wants all of his readers to ask themselves whether they too will

be among those who betray a messiah who chooses to suffer and die in obedience to God's call.

When people come to arrest Jesus and someone tries to defend him with a sword, Jesus reminds all those who are present (and the reader) that he is not a "bandit"—that is, not a "messiah," as the term was sometimes understood. In the first century, many would-be messiahs were bandits.

This section emphasizes that even those disciples who want to suffer with Jesus fail completely. Led by Peter, the eleven all insist that they will die rather than deny Jesus. Yet, immediately thereafter, they are not even able to stay awake and pray. Then when Judas and the authorities arrive, the disciples flee. The final scene of the young man dressed in linen symbolizes the abject failure of the disciples who want to share in Jesus' passion. We read that the young man was "also following with him," and that tells the readers that we should think of him as one of Jesus' students, and, since he is present at the time of the arrest, we also should think of him as someone who at least aspires to the way of the cross. Nevertheless, the young man flees away naked, and within Jewish and early Christian culture to flee naked was the ultimate sign of humiliating defeat (cf. Amos 2:16, Acts 19:16).

The reason the students fail despite their sincerity is that they do not watch and pray. Mark stresses that their intentions are good. As Jesus notes, their spirits are "eager." However, because their "flesh is weak," they do not persevere in watchful prayer. While Jesus is struggling with God's bitter will for him, they repeatedly go to sleep. Therefore, when the hour of temptation comes, they fall away.

The failure of the disciples serves as a poignant warning to Mark's readers. Earlier in the gospel, Mark warns us that a time of testing is at hand and we must be ready. We first receive this admonition in Mark's interpretation of the Parable of the Sower. The seed which landed on the rock, sprang up and then withered represents those who initially receive the word with joy but later fall away when persecution comes (4:5–6, 16–17). Of course, the warnings become especially shrill in chapter 13 when Jesus describes in detail the time of supreme crisis. At the conclusion of that discourse, Jesus repeatedly tells us to "watch." Indeed, Jesus' last words are, "What I say to you, I say to all, watch!" (13:36). Hence, when Mark subsequently describes how the disciples disregard similar warnings in Gethsemane and so end up deserting Jesus, he is reminding the reader of what will happen to us if we aspire to the way of the cross and yet refuse to wait and pray.

Questions for Reflection:

Are people who are the most enthusiastic about following Jesus often the ones who are least ready to wait and pray? As a result, do such people sometimes fall away in times of stress, whereas other Christians remain firm? Why are enthusiastic people often unrealistic about their own weaknesses? Are some people today prepared to defend Jesus with armed force? What would Mark say to such people?

38.   Mark 14:53–72

And they led Jesus away to the high priest, and all the chief priests and the elders and the scribes came together. And Peter from a distance followed him as far as the interior of the high priest's courtyard and was sitting in the firelight along with the retainers and warming himself. And the chief priests and the whole council were seeking testimony against Jesus to put him to death, and they were not finding any. For many testified falsely against him, but their testimonies were not consistent. And some rose and testified falsely against him saying, "We ourselves heard him saying, 'I will destroy this sanctuary made with hands, and in three days I will build another not made with hands.'" And not even so was their testimony consistent. And the high priest rose in the middle and asked Jesus, "Aren't you going to answer anything? What are these people testifying against you?" But he was silent and did not answer anything. Again the high priest questioned him by saying to him, "Are you the Messiah, the Son of the Blessed?" And Jesus said, "I am, and you will see the son of humanity sitting on the right of the Power and coming with the clouds of heaven." And the high priest ripped his clothes and said, "Why do we still have need of witnesses? You heard the blasphemy. What do you think?" And they all condemned him to be guilty of a capital offense. And some began to spit on him and to blindfold his face and to hit him and to say to him, "Prophesy!" and the retainers welcomed him with blows (14:53–65).

And while Peter was below in the courtyard, one of the high priest's maids came and, after she noticed Peter warming himself, she looked at him and said, "You too were with the Nazarene Jesus." But he denied it by saying, "I neither know nor understand what you are saying." And he went out into the forecourt, and the cock crowed. And after the maid noticed him, she began again to say to the bystanders, "This is one of them." And he again kept denying it, and after a little while the bystanders again said to Peter, "Surely you are one of them, for you too are a Galilean." And he began to bind himself by a curse and swear, "I do not know this person you are mentioning." And at once the cock crowed a second time. And Peter was reminded of the words that Jesus said to him, "Before the cock crows twice, you will disown me three times." And he began to weep (14:66–72).

Mark carefully connects Jesus' trial and Peter's denial. Mark begins the section by noting both that the retainers led away Jesus to the high priest's residence and that Peter followed from a distance and entered into the courtyard. In line with this introduction, we next have Jesus' trial and condemnation and then Peter's denial.

Thematically, this section reverses Peter's confession in chapter 8. In that scene Peter responds to the question of who Jesus is by declaring that he is the Messiah. Of course, Jesus tells him not to divulge this publicly because Jesus and his followers must suffer. Now Jesus himself responds to the question of who he is by declaring that he is the Messiah. Meanwhile, Peter is denying that he knows Jesus.

Taken together, these scenes make it evident that a theme of Mark's gospel is that before we can confess that Jesus is the Messiah, we must confess in word and deed that he is the one who suffered. Here, Jesus confesses publicly that he is the Christ, but he does so to insure that he will suffer. Mark emphasizes that, if Jesus does not publicly confess that he is the Messiah, he will not suffer. Despite the best efforts of the high priests and their retainers, they cannot secure a conviction without Jesus' cooperation. The testimony of the false witnesses is inconsistent, and the case against Jesus is falling apart. In desperation, the high priest turns to Jesus. If Jesus merely continues to remain silent, he will go free. At this point, Jesus chooses to declare he is the Messiah, and he does so to guarantee that he will endure torture and death! By contrast, earlier in the gospel when Peter confesses that Jesus is the Messiah, Jesus tells him not to make the fact known. We soon learn why. When Jesus announces that he must suffer, Peter objects. Now Peter's unwillingness to suffer makes him deny that he knows Jesus at the precise moment when Jesus himself proclaims publicly he is the Messiah.

To help make it clear that Jesus is the suffering Messiah, Mark carefully balances the title of Messiah with the title "son of humanity." The chief priest asks whether Jesus is the "Messiah." Jesus answers, "I am," but then immediately goes on to speak of himself as the "son of humanity." As son of humanity, he will suffer in this world and then reign over the age to come.

Probably, Mark also intends to remind his readers that, as "Son of God." Jesus exercises divine authority and that they will soon face his judgment. The high priest asks Jesus whether he is the "Messiah, the Son of the Blessed." Here, the "Blessed" is God. Apparently, for the high priest, the titles "Messiah" and "Son of God" are synonymous, but they are not for Mark. Significantly, in response to the high priest's question concerning who he is, Jesus replies, "I am," and, of course, that phrase belongs, properly speaking, to God alone (cf. Exod 3:14). This divine Jesus is the one whom not only the high priest but also Mark's readers will soon "see" at the final judgment.

Questions for Reflection:

> For us, is the fact that Peter denied Jesus a warning or a comfort or both? Do Christians sometimes try to confess Jesus prematurely, before they learn what the cost of following Jesus is? Did the high priest really think that Jesus committed blasphemy? Why?

39.   Mark 15:1–27

And as soon as it was day, the chief priests, after consulting with the elders and scribes and the whole Sanhedrin, tied up Jesus and took him off and handed him over to Pilate. And Pilate asked him, "You are the king of the Jews?" But he in reply said to him, "That is the way you would say it." And the chief priests kept accusing him of many things. And Pilate asked him again, "Aren't you going to answer anything? See how much they are accusing you of." But Jesus no longer made any answer, so that Pilate was amazed (15:1–5).

Each festival, he used to release for them one prisoner, whomever they requested. Now there was a man called Barabbas who was bound with the rebels who had committed murder in the revolt. And the crowd came up and began to ask him to do what he normally did for them. And Pilate answered them, "Do you want me to release for you the 'king of the Jews'?" For he knew that the chief priests had handed him over out of jealousy. But the chief priests stirred up the crowd so he would release Barabbas for them instead. Pilate replying back said to them, "So what am I to do with the 'king of the Jews'?" They shouted back, "Crucify him." But Pilate said to them, "Why? What evil did he do?" But they shouted vehemently, "Crucify him." And Pilate, desiring to satisfy the crowd, released Barabbas for them, and he whipped Jesus and handed him over to be crucified (15:6–15).

And the soldiers led him away inside the courtyard, that is the Praetorium, and they called together the whole cohort. And they dressed him in purple, and they wove a crown from thorns and put it on him. And they began to greet him, "Hail, king of the Jews!" And they beat his head with a stick and spat on him and bent their knees and worshipped him. And when they had ridiculed him, they stripped him of the purple and put his own clothes on him. And they led him out to crucify him (15:16–20).

And they pressed into service a passer-by, a certain Simon of Cyrene, who was coming from the countryside, the father of Alexander and Rufus, to carry his cross. And they brought him to a place, Golgotha, which translated means, "Skull Place." And they tried to give him wine flavored with myrrh. But he did not take it. And they crucified him. And they divided up his garments by casting lots over them to determine who would take away what. And it was the third hour when they crucified him. And there was a superscription of the charge against him, reading, "The king of the Jews." And with him they crucified two bandits, one on his right and one on his left (15:21–27).

In this section, Mark carefully explains to his readers in what sense Jesus is the "Messiah." Mark invites us to consider this question in the opening dialogue between Pilate and Jesus. In Pilate's question, "You are the king of the Jews?" the *you* is emphatic. Hence, the words already push us to wonder how it can be appropriate to think of this particular individual as a king. Jesus' answer also contains an emphatic *you* and so is perhaps best translated: "That is the way you would say it." Accordingly, Mark suggests that Pilate's words are only partially true. As the narrative continues, it insists that the words are true in the sense that Jesus fulfills the prophecies of the Hebrew Scriptures. Thus, we have repeated allusions to many texts. For example, the soldiers dividing up Jesus' clothes reflects Ps 22:18. By contrast, Mark implies that it is false to say Jesus is a king if we take the declaration to mean that Jesus is willing to use force to achieve earthly glory. On the contrary, Jesus refuses even to defend himself before Pilate. Instead, like the suffering servant in Isa 53:7, he is silent in the face of injustice. The contrast between Jesus' suffering kingship and the kingship of this world becomes unmistakable when Pilate asks the crowds to choose between Jesus and Barabbas. Barabbas is a revolutionary who committed murder. He is someone who used violence in an attempt to become an earthly king. Significantly, in the narrative Barabbas does not have to suffer and die. Then the nature of Jesus' kingship becomes brutally evident when the soldiers ridicule Jesus. As the soldiers salute Jesus as "king" and abuse him, Mark invites the reader to realize that Jesus' kingship is of a different order than what the soldiers mean by "king."

Questions for Reflection:

In what sense can we say that Jesus is a king? How did Jesus' kingship become especially visible in his trial, mocking, and crucifixion?

40.   Mark 15:29-32

And the passers-by reviled him, shaking their heads and saying, "Ha! You who are going to destroy the sanctuary and build it in three days, save yourself by coming down from the cross." Likewise, the chief priests, along with the scribes, also ridiculed him to one another and kept saying, "He saved others; he cannot save himself. Let the Messiah, Israel's King, come down now from the cross so we can see and believe." And those who were crucified with him taunted him (15:29–32).

In this section, Mark brings to a climax his themes that Jesus does not work miracles to avoid suffering and that miracles do not produce real faith. Jesus' enemies taunt him to work a miracle. However, if he had complied, he would have used miracles to escape suffering and death. As we have seen throughout the gospel, Jesus never uses miracles in this way. On the contrary, Jesus deliberately works miracles which lead to suffering and death. Similarly, Jesus' enemies claim that if only he will work a miraculous sign, they will believe in him. Earlier in the gospel, the Pharisees also test Jesus by demanding that he work a heavenly sign, and he refuses (8:11–12). Such signs would not produce the faith which Mark requires. If Jesus did come down from the cross, what the chief priests would believe is that he is "Israel's King." However, Jesus is not "Israel's King" in the sense that they mean. Ironically, Jesus' enemies assume that his failure to work a miracle is a judgment on him, whereas, in fact, it is a judgment on them.

Questions for Reflection:

Does God sometimes show his goodness and power by choosing not to work a miracle? Are people's attacks on Jesus or the church sometimes a judgment on themselves?

41.   Mark 15:33-36

And when the sixth hour came, darkness fell on the whole land until the ninth hour. And at the ninth hour Jesus shouted with a great cry, "Eloi, Eloi, lema sabachthani?" which is translated, "My God, my God, for what reason have you abandoned me?" And some of the bystanders heard and said, "See, he is calling Elijah." And one ran, filled a sponge with wine vinegar, put it around a stick, and let him drink and said, "So, let us see if Elijah is coming to take him down" (15:33-36).

This section is difficult and has prompted much speculation. There has been a great deal of discussion about the significance of Jesus' question as to why God has abandoned him. No less perplexing is the bystanders' conclusion that Jesus is calling on Elijah.

For Mark's intended readers, however, the passage primarily continues the theme that Jesus fulfills the scriptures by dying. The question, "My God, my God, for what reason have you abandoned me?" is the opening of Psalm 22, and Mark has alluded to this psalm earlier (Mark 15:24; Ps 22:18). Jesus being given vinegar to drink recalls another scriptural passage, Ps 69:21. Both passages stress the suffering which a righteous person undergoes at the hands of the wicked. Jesus as the supremely righteous one who suffers at the hands of the utterly wicked fulfills these passages.

I suspect Mark hoped that the discussion about the coming of Elijah would remind readers that Jesus is the son of humanity who is coming. As we have noted before, Mark does not let the title of "Messiah" stand alone. Instead, he supplements it with the titles "son of humanity" and "Son of God." For example, in chapter 8 when Peter proclaims Jesus is the "Messiah," Jesus talks about the "son of humanity," and in the next scene, a voice from heaven declares that Jesus is God's Son (9:7). In the gospel, Mark looks forward to the coming of the "son of humanity" and links it with the coming of Elijah. Thus, in chapter 9, Jesus reassures the disciples that Elijah will indeed come first, but that Elijah (John the Baptist) and the "son of humanity" both must suffer (9:11–13). Therefore, when the bystanders discuss whether Elijah will come to deliver Jesus, the reader might well recall that Jesus is the "son of humanity" who is coming.

Questions for Reflection:

How does Jesus fulfill biblical texts, such as Psalm 22 and Psalm 69, that were not prophecies in the strict sense? Can we who are "sons" and daughters "of humanity" fulfill such texts too? In what sense is it true to say that God abandonned Jesus on the cross?

42.   Mark 15:37–39

But Jesus let out a great cry and expired. And the curtain of the sanctuary was torn in two, from the top down to the bottom. And when the centurion who stood by facing him saw that he expired in this way, he said, "Truly this person was God's Son" (15:37–39).

Here, Mark brings his Christology to its climax by suggesting that through his death Jesus has abolished the barrier that separates God from humanity. When Jesus dies, the curtain of the sanctuary is torn in two. The curtain separated the place where God symbolically dwelt from the places where his

Jewish worshippers could be. The temple in turn separated the God of Israel and his chosen people from Pagans. Once the curtain is destroyed, God is fully visible and available to all. This new situation becomes evident when the Roman centurion—presumably, a Pagan—immediately declares that Jesus is God's Son. Significantly, all this occurs when Jesus dies.

Literarily, this scene complements the scene at Jesus' baptism and stresses that his mission is now fulfilled. At the beginning of the gospel, John the Baptist proclaims that his successor will baptize with the Holy Spirit. Jesus appears and is baptized himself. The heavens are "torn" open, Jesus receives the Holy Spirit, and a voice from heaven declares that he is God's Son. However, apparently no one but Jesus hears the heavenly voice, and, subsequently, Jesus does not in fact baptize with the Holy Spirit. Now, at the gospel's climax, the veil of the temple is "torn" apart and for the first time a human being declares that Jesus is God's Son. Hence, thanks to Jesus' death, the world has at last received God's message, and we are confident that the Holy Spirit will soon be available to everyone.

In this climactic scene, Mark emphasizes to his readers that we can only learn who Jesus is by focusing on the cross. Previously, no person in the gospel ever confesses that Jesus is God's Son. This failure is all the more noteworthy because first the demons and then God himself declare to various bystanders who Jesus actually is. Now, however, a Roman soldier who never had the benefit of such supernatural testimony confesses, "Truly this person was God's Son." Mark explicitly tells us that the centurion said this when he saw how Jesus died.

Questions for Reflection:

Is it true that people can learn who Jesus is only by focusing on the cross? Why? Why did Jesus have to die before he could baptize his followers with the Holy Spirit?

⇥ ✻ ⇤

43.   Mark 15:40 – 16:8

Now there were also women who watched from a distance. Among them were Mary Magdalene and Mary, the mother of the younger James and Joses, and Salome (these followed him when he was in Galilee and provided for him). And many other women who had come up to Jerusalem with him were present (15:40–41).

And when evening had already begun, since it was the day of preparation (that is, the day before the Sabbath), Joseph of Arimathea came. He was a prominent member of the Sanhedrin who also himself was awaiting God's rule. He dared to come to Pilate and asked for Jesus' body. Pilate wondered if he had already died, and he summoned the centurion and asked him if he had been dead long. And when he found out from the centurion, he granted the corpse to Joseph. And he bought a piece of linen and took him down and wrapped him in the linen and put him in a tomb which was hewn from rock, and he rolled a stone to the entrance of the tomb. And Mary Magdalene and Mary the mother of Joses noticed where he was put (15:42–47).

And when the Sabbath had passed, Mary Magdalene, Mary the mother of James, and Salome bought spices so they could come and anoint him. And very early on the first day of the week, they came to the tomb after the sun rose. And they said to each other, "Who will roll away for us the stone from the entrance of the tomb?" And they looked up and noticed that the stone had been rolled away, for it was extremely big. And they went into the tomb and saw a young man sitting on the right, dressed in a white robe, and they were astounded. But he said to them, "Do not be astounded. You are seeking Jesus of Nazareth who was crucified. He has been raised; he is not here. See the place where they put him. But go off, say to his students and to Peter, 'He is going ahead of you into Galilee. There you will see him, just as he said to you.'"

And they came out and fled from the tomb, for trembling and confusion gripped them, and they said nothing to anyone, for they were afraid (16:1–8).

To readers who are familiar with other gospels, this ending is startling. Matthew, Luke, and John go on to include stories of the risen Jesus appearing to his followers. Hence, it seems strange to us that Mark does not, especially since earlier Jesus tells his students that they will see him in Galilee (cf. 14:28), and now the young man at the tomb repeats this promise.

Most of the surviving manuscripts of Mark do go on to give us accounts of resurrection appearances, but these are later additions. The earliest and best manuscripts lack them, and, if these stories came from Mark himself, it is impossible to explain why ancient scribes would have omitted them.

We must suppose that when Mark wrote the gospel the original ending was less startling. Since the other gospels did not yet exist, readers did not have any expectation concerning how such a book should end. Moreover, at this early date it was obvious that the title was "The Beginning of the Good News of Jesus the Messiah, God's Son" (1:1), and this title suggested that Mark would only narrate the first part of the story.

By breaking off the narrative before the disciples see Jesus again, Mark was able to make the crucifixion the climax of the gospel. Had Mark gone on to describe a triumphant encounter between the risen Christ and his followers, this resurrection scene would inevitably have become the climax, and Mark's focus on the cross would have been compromised.

To Mark's original readers, the young man dressed in white would have suggested the ultimate triumph of the believer when we will reign with Jesus in glory. To be sure, the "young man ... dressed in a white robe" is an angel. Still, it is significant that Mark does not call him an angel. Earlier in Mark's gospel, Jesus declares that in the resurrection the faithful are "like angels"

(12:25), and the Apocalypse tells us that in eternal life the saved wear "white robes" (Rev 6:11, 7:9, etc.). In chapter 14:51–52 we have a young man who symbolizes the failure of those who follow Jesus; now we have a "young man" who proclaims the resurrection and so symbolizes our final victory.

Nevertheless, even for its original readers, Mark's gospel must have ended on a disconcerting note. The faithful women who bury Jesus cannot deal with the terrifying news that he has risen from the dead. As a result, they disobey the heavenly messenger and tell no one what they heard.

This ending brings to a climax the theme that the students of Jesus have failed. Earlier in the gospel, all the disciples who have previously been mentioned fail. Judas betrays Jesus, Peter denies him, the rest flee. However, when he narrates the burial of Jesus, Mark introduces some more disciples, and initially these appear to be faithful. Mark tells us that Joseph of Arimathea "dared" to go to Pilate to obtain Jesus' body and bury it. Significantly, Mark tells us that Joseph "was awaiting God's rule," i.e., that he is a disciple. Mark also tells up about the women who watch Jesus' death and go to the tomb to anoint his body. Mark emphasizes that they too are disciples. They "followed" Jesus, provided for him in Galilee, and accompanied him to Jerusalem. However, at the supreme moment when they receive the command to share the news, they become afraid and remain silent.

Consequently, Mark's gospel ends with a warning to the reader to do better. Earlier, we noted that in the gospel Peter is an example of what the reader must avoid. In chapter 13, Jesus talks about the crisis which Mark's own readers must endure and warns them to "watch." Then, in the garden of Gethsamene, Jesus commands Peter to watch, and yet he falls asleep. Subsequently, Peter denies knowing Jesus. So too, the women serve as a warning. We must not be so afraid in the midst of the crisis of our own time that we refuse to proclaim the resurrection.

Despite everything, however, the gospel ends on a note of hope. Even if the disciples have failed, Jesus has triumphed. He has risen from the dead. He is going before his followers to Galilee. There they will see him. Even Peter who denied him will see him. Jesus will give them new power and a greater mission. So too, Mark's readers know that Jesus still lives and reigns. Indeed, Mark proclaims that soon Jesus will return in glory to reward those who have remained faithful. The words of the angel are equally addressed to the readers of the gospel, "You will see him, just as he said to you."

Questions for Reflection:

In how many ways was the prophecy that the disciples would "see" Jesus fulfilled? In how many ways does Mark's gospel invite us to "see" Jesus today?

Appendix

Producing an Outline of Mark's Gospel

M ost modern commentaries on Mark outline the gospel. They first divide the text into major sections (e.g., "Mark 8:27–10:52: The Journey to Jerusalem"). Then, they divide these into smaller units (e.g., "Mark 10:32–45: The Third Passion Prediction") and subunits (e.g., "Mark 10:32–34: Jesus Predicts his Death").

In addition, some modern printings of the actual text of Mark break up the gospel into sections and provide summarizing titles for each. Indeed, even the standard modern edition of Mark's original Greek (published by the United Bible Societies) does this.

By contrast, a minority of modern scholars have argued that outlines and summarizing titles are inappropriate. Mark's gospel is a seamless web whose themes crisscross in highly complex ways, and it is misleading to divide up the text or to draw special attention to only one dimension of a passage which contains many. Just as it would destroy the beautiful patterns of an oriental carpet to cut it up into strips, so dividing up Mark and labeling the individual sections ruins our perception of the whole.

In the original Greek text of Mark, there were no breaks at all. Typically, ancient manuscripts have no section titles or paragraphs. Indeed, they do not even have punctuation or space between words. All there is is an uninterrupted series of individual letters!

Naturally, however, when an ancient person read the gospel out loud to the Christian assembly, there must have been breaks between smaller units and perhaps even indications of larger structural features. Certainly, for example, the reader paused

111

at the end of sentences. Readers who had training in rhetoric or drama—as so many people in the ancient world did—might have used differing inflections of their voices to help the audience make thematic connections between various parts of the gospel (e.g., the three passion predictions in Mark 8–10).

Any good modern outline of the gospel must respect the overriding structural features. Clearly, there are in Mark crucial transitions, important refrains, and other dominant literary indications. Thus, for example, it is hard to deny that the gospel's plot takes a major turn when Peter confesses that Jesus is the Messiah and Jesus replies that he must suffer (8:27ff.). Another major turn occurs when Jesus actually arrives in the vicinity of Jerusalem where the suffering will take place (11:1ff.). Accordingly, any outline should indicate such central structures.

At the same time, however, anyone who attempts to outline Mark must sometimes choose to highlight certain themes and other features at the expense of equally important ones. Part of the genius of Mark is that he was able to use the same material to be part of multiple structures. Thus, for example, in the commentary I argued that the two-stage healing of the blind man in 8:22–26 has two very different literary functions. On the one hand, it points forward to the two great confessions to Jesus which follow immediately. When Peter confesses that Jesus is the Messiah but should not have to suffer, he sees only partially. Full sight is confessing that Jesus is God's Son, a confession which soon follows. Nevertheless, the same two-stage healing continues the pattern of declining miracles due to declining faith. The healing of the blind man is more difficult than the preceding healing (7:31–37) and less difficult than the subsequent one (9:14–29). In the context of a single outline, however, a person cannot honor both literary functions of the miracle and so must choose the one he or she decides is more significant.

Because any outline must highlight some themes and other features at the expense of equally important ones, no single outline can be definitive, and in fact many different ones are helpful. The number of scholarly outlines of Mark is practically as great as the number of scholars. This abundance is a testimony to the richness of Mark and the importance of highlighting different parts of the web of inner connections.

At this point, it might be a useful exercise for the reader to produce a personal outline of Mark. In this little commentary, I have pointed out the most important literary structures and also tried to indicate some of the web of inner connections. In the actual translation, I have shown where I feel such things as paragraph breaks might be. I now invite my readers to come up with their own outlines. I predict that, at least in many details, the resulting outlines will all be different, but probably none of them will be "wrong." By comparing such outlines, readers will gain a greater sense of the beauty and complexity of Mark's gospel and have more appreciation for both the insight and limitations of what I have written.

After completing their own outlines, readers might be interested in comparing them with mine.

An Outline of Mark's Gospel

I.   Title: The Beginning of the Good News of Jesus the Messiah, God's Son (1:1).

II. Prologue: Jesus is God's Son who will baptize with the Holy Spirit but who first must suffer (1:2–13).
     A.   John the Baptist announces the coming of the mighty one who will baptize with the Holy Spirit (1:2–8).
     B.   Jesus receives the Holy Spirit, and God declares that Jesus is his Son but in so doing indicates that Jesus must suffer (1:9–11). Then Satan tests Jesus (1:12–13).

III. Part 1: Jesus begins his ministry of preparation for God's rule and hides his identity as God's Son (1:14–3:12).
   A. Jesus begins his ministry of preparation (1:14–20).
      1. He proclaims that God's rule has drawn near and that people must repent (1:14–15).
      2. He calls four students and tells them that one day he will make them fishers of human beings (1:16–20).
   B. Jesus silences demons who attempt to reveal that he is God's Son and tries to avoid public acclaim for his miracles (1:21–45).
      1. Jesus casts out and silences a demon who declares he is "God's holy one" (1:21–28).
      2. Jesus heals Simon's mother–in–law privately (1:29–31).
      3. Jesus casts out many demons and does not let them reveal who he is (1:32–34).
      4. Jesus insists on going elsewhere when everyone is looking for him (1:35–39).
      5. Jesus heals a leper and orders him not to publicize the miracle, and when the leper does, Jesus withdraws to the desert (1:40–45).
   C. Jesus publicly incites opposition and proclaims he is a human being (2:1–3:6).
      1. Jesus publicly heals a paralytic and insists that as a "human being" he has the power to forgive sins. Consequently, the scribes become concerned (2:1–12).
      2. Jesus associates with tax collectors and sinners and so provokes the scribes and Pharisees (2:13–17).
      3. Jesus defends his students for their unorthodox custom of not fasting and, apparently, irritates the disciples of John and those of the Pharisees. Jesus identifies himself as the "bridegroom" (2:18–22).
      4. Jesus defends his students for picking grain on the Sabbath and so irritates the Pharisees. Jesus insists that as a "human being" he is Lord of the Sabbath (2:23–28).
      5. Jesus heals a man on the Sabbath, prompting the Pharisees and Herodians to plot to kill him (3:1–6).
   D. Summary: Jesus tries to escape public attention and refuses to let the demons reveal that he is God's Son (3:7–12).

IV. Part 2: Jesus continues his ministry of preparation by telling his students that they must patiently endure and that they can trust him. However, they fail to understand (3:13–8:21 [or 8:26]).

   A. Jesus selects his students, and they are his true family.
1. Jesus chooses the twelve to share his ministry (3:13–19).
2. His relatives and the scribes assume Jesus is possessed, and Jesus denies it (3:20–30).
3. Jesus declares that his true family are those who do God's will (3:31–35).

   B. Jesus tells his students the secret that his followers must patiently suffer as they wait for the full coming of God's rule (4:1–34).
1. Jesus tells the parable of the sower and explains privately to his students that it means they must endure with patience (4:1–25).
   a. Jesus tells the Parable of the Sower to the crowd (4:1–9).
   b. He informs his students that he uses parables so outsiders will not understand (4:10–12).
   c. He explains to his students that the parable teaches that only those who endure will bear fruit (4:13–20).
   d. He indicates that later outsiders will also learn the meaning (4:21–23).
   e. He warns his students to pay attention to what he has taught them (4:24–25).
2. Jesus tells parables which indicate that God's rule will come later (4:26–33).
   a. The Parable of the Seed That Grows by Itself (4:26–29).
   b. The Parable of the Mustard Seed (4:30–32).
3. Summary: Jesus tells parables to outsiders and explains the meaning to his students (4:33–34).

   C. Jesus works a series of miracles whose message is that we must have faith in him (4:35–6:6a).
1. The Stilling of the Storm. Jesus challenges his students to trust him despite danger, since he exercises the power of God (4:35–41).

2. The Exorcism of the Gerasene Demoniac. Jesus works
    a miracle which frightens the villagers, and they ask
    him to leave (5:1–20).

3. Two miracles contrasting trust and distrust (5:21–43).
    a. The Healing of the Hemorrhaging Woman. The
        woman trusts Jesus' power to heal her, and Je-
        sus insists on bringing the miracle to public at-
        tention (5:24b–34).
    b. The Raising of Jairus's Daughter. People do not
        trust that Jesus can raise the dead, and so
        when he works the miracle, Jesus insists that it
        should not be publicized (5:21–24a, 35–43).

4. Jesus works a few miracles in Nazareth and marvels at
    the lack of faith (6:1–6a).

D. Jesus teaches his students that their mission will be difficult
    (6:6b–6:30).
    1. Jesus sends the twelve out to preach and tells them
        they must go empty-handed and be aware that they
        may not be received. They go out, work, and re-
        turn (6:7–13, 30).
    2. John the Baptist is executed for preaching God's word
        (6:14–29).

E. Jesus works a series of miracles in which he again chal-
    lenges his students to recognize that he has divine power
    and so they should trust him and persevere. However,
    they fail to understand (6:31–56).
    1. The feeding of the five thousand. Jesus challenges his
        students to feed the multitude, and he then takes
        what they have and enables them to do so
        (6:31–44).
    2. The walking on water. Jesus sends his students into a
        difficult situation and then saves them by his divine
        power, but they fail to understand (6:45–52).
    3. The healing of many sick in Gennesaret. The people
        show the faith his students lack (6:53–56).

F. Jesus teaches that lack of faith is what truly defiles (7:1–30).
    1. The hypocritical tradition of the elders. Jesus teaches
        his students that real sin comes from within and in-
        cludes foolish unbelief (7:1–23).

2. The healing of the Syrophoenician woman's daughter. Jesus responds to the woman's persistent faith despite the fact that she is ritually unclean (7:24–30).

G. Due to other people's lack of faith, Jesus has difficulty working miracles and insists that they be kept secret (7:31–8:26).

    1. The healing of the deaf and dumb man. Jesus has difficulty working the miracle and insists that it not be publicized (7:31–37).

    2. The feeding of the four thousand. Jesus dismisses the crowd to keep them from perceiving the miracle. The disciples still have no trust in Jesus, and the miracle is less than the previous feeding (8:1–10).

    3. The Pharisees in their skepticism demand a sign from Jesus, but he refuses to give one (8:11–13).

    4. Conclusion: The disciples' hearts are hardened through lack of faith, and so the miracles are decreasing (8:14–21).

    5. Transitional giving of sight story: Jesus has to heal a blind man twice, and he orders the man to avoid talking to anyone (8:22–26). This story also symbolizes the growth in understanding noted below.

V. Part 3: Jesus tells his students plainly that he is God's Son and he and they must suffer, but they do not respond positively (8:27–10:52).

A. Jesus plainly tells his students for the first time that he is God's Son and both he and they must suffer.

    1. Peter's confession and the first passion prediction, negative reaction, and teaching (8:27–9:1).

       a. In response to Jesus' question, Peter proclaims that Jesus is the Messiah (8:27–29).

       b. Jesus responds by saying openly that he must suffer. Peter reacts negatively, and Jesus reprimands him (8:30–33).

       c. Jesus tells people that his followers must suffer in order to be saved (8:34–9:1).

    2. The Transfiguration (9:2–13). Jesus reveals to Peter, James, and John that he is God's Son, but orders them not to tell anyone until the resurrection. Jesus

like John the Baptist must suffer. The three disciples react with confusion.

B. The healing of the demon–possessed boy. The least possible faith makes the miracle as difficult as possible (9:14–29). The time for miracles has now passed.

C. Second passion prediction, negative reaction, and teaching (9:30–37).
   1. Jesus predicts his execution and resurrection, but his students do not understand (9:30–32).
   2. The disciples discuss which of them is the greatest (9:33–34).
   3. Jesus teaches that whoever wishes to be first must be last and what we do to the least in the community we do to Jesus (9:35–37).

D. Jesus gives an outline of how Christians should serve various members of his fellowship (9:38–10:31). We must:
   1. Be charitable to outsiders who do not harm us (9:38–41).
   2. Avoid hurting the defenseless believer, lest we be cast into Gehenna (9:42–50).
   3. Not divorce one another (10:1–12).
   4. Receive little children (10:13–16).
   5. Give up our wealth (10:17–27).
   6. Summary: Christians are a single family in which the first must be the last (10:28–31).

E. The third passion prediction, negative reaction, and teaching (10:32–45).
   1. Jesus predicts his death in detail (10:32–34).
   2. James and John ask for the seats of honor in the kingdom, and the ten become angry (10:35–41).
   3. Jesus teaches that whoever wants to be first must be last, in imitation of the self–sacrifice of Jesus himself (10:42–45).

VI. Part 4: Jesus begins to reveal his identity to the world and incites attempts to destroy him (10:46 [or 11:1]–12:44).

A. Transitional giving of sight story. Bartimaeus proclaims that Jesus is the Son of David. Jesus refuses to let him be silenced. Jesus heals him of his blindness, and Bartimaeus follows him "on the road" (10:46–52).

B. Jesus acts as God's anointed and provokes a plot against him (11:1–25).
   1. Jesus stages a triumphal journey toward Jerusalem, and the crowds proclaim the coming of David's kingdom (11:1–11).
   2. Jesus cleanses the temple and curses the fig tree whose destruction foreshadows the temple's. As a result, the religious authorities want to arrest Jesus (11:12–25).
C. A series of controversy stories about Jesus' authority. These suggest he is God's Son (11:27–12:37).
   1. Introduction: The religious leaders demand to know the source of Jesus' authority, and he suggests his authority comes from the same place as John's (i.e., "from heaven") (11:27–33).
   2. Jesus tells the Parable of the Wicked Tenants (12:1–12). The parable suggests that Jesus is God's Son, and the authorities try to arrest him.
   3. The Pharisees and Herodians fail to trap Jesus with a question about taxes (12:13–17).
   4. The Sadducees fail to discredit Jesus with a question about the resurrection (12:18–27).
   5. The question about the great commandment. Jesus' answer silences his critics (12:28–34).
   6. Conclusion: Jesus hints to his critics that the Messiah is in reality God's Son (12:35–37).
D. Jesus denounces the scribes for their greed and praises the widow for her generosity (12:38–44).

VII. Part 5: Jesus foretells in detail the suffering of his followers and warns them not to be deceived by the false prophets who work miracles. Instead, they must be faithful as they await the end (13:1–37).
   A. Introduction.
      1. In response to a comment by a disciple, Jesus predicts the destruction of the temple (13:1–2).
      2. Peter, James, John, and Andrew ask privately when this will take place (13:3–4).
   B. Jesus' prophecy (13:5–37).
      1. Introduction: Jesus warns against the false prophets (13:5–6).

2.   The sufferings of his followers prior to the great tribulation (13:7–13).
3.   The tribulation and warnings against following the false prophets who work miracles (13:14–23).
4.   The end of the world and the coming of the son of humanity (13:24–27).
5.   Jesus tells that the time is soon but unknown; so we must watch (13:28–37).

VIII. Part 6: Jesus is acclaimed God's Son as he suffers and dies (14:1–15:39). The disciples fail to be faithful.
    A.   As the authorities and Judas plot against Jesus, a woman anoints him (14:1–11).
    B.   The last supper (14:12–26).
       1.   Preparations for the supper (14:12–16).
       2.   At supper Jesus announces the betrayal (14:17–21).
       3.   The institution of the eucharist (14:22–25).
       4.   Jesus and his students depart for the Mount of Olives (14:26).
    C.   Jesus predicts Peter's denial (14:27–31).
    D.   Jesus prays for strength in Gethsemane while the disciples sleep (14:32–42).
    E.   The betrayal and arrest and the flight of the disciples (14:43–52).
    F.   The hearing before the high priest. Jesus proclaims he is God's Son and is condemned to death for blasphemy. Meanwhile, Peter denies knowing Jesus (14:53–72).
    G.   The trial before Pilate. Pilate condemns Jesus for being the King of the Jews (15:1–15).
    H.   The soldiers ironically acclaim Jesus as king (15:16–20).
    I.   The crucifixion. The world ironically acclaims Jesus as king (15:21–27).
    J.   The bystanders dare Jesus to work a miracle to save himself and make them believe (15:29–32).
    K.   The death of Jesus. The curtain of the sanctuary is torn, and the centurion declares that Jesus is God's Son (15:33–39).

IX. Epilogue (15:40–16:8).
    A.   Jesus' burial (15:40–47).
    B.   The women go to the tomb and learn that Jesus has risen, but fail to share the news (16:1–8).

Notes

1. Fowler takes the more radical view that Mark himself composed the feeding of the five thousand on the model of the feeding of the four thousand. R.M. Fowler, *Loaves and Fishes: The Function of the Feeding Stories in the Gospel of Mark* (Chico, CA: Scholars Press, 1981).

2. L. William Countryman, "How Many Baskets Full? Mark 8:14–21 and the Value of Miracles in Mark,"*Catholic Biblical Quarterly* 47 (1985):643–55.

3. Other details in the two feedings also suggest decline. Thus, in the first story Jesus starts with only two fish (6:41) and feeds five thousand men, whereas in the second, he starts with a few fish (8:7) and feeds four thousand (with no suggestion that they were only men). To be sure, in the second story Mark uses a word which can mean "little fish." However, the word also means simply "fish." It is harder to know whether the different terms Mark uses for "basket" point to a decline, since both wicker and mat baskets came in various sizes. Wicker baskets were normally stronger than mat baskets, and so perhaps when the two terms were set side by side, an ancient reader might have assumed the wicker baskets were larger, just as we might assume that a "hamper" would normally be bigger than a "basket." For a discussion of the different words for "basket" see F.J.A. Hort, "A Note by the Late Dr Hort on the Words kophinos, spuris, sargane,"*The Journal of Theological Studies* 10 (1909):567–71.

4. By the "reader" Mark especially means the person who would read the book to the Christian assembly. It was important for him or her to be informed, because after the reading, the congregation might ask questions or make comments.

Other Titles Available from BIBAL Press

Prices subject to change

Postage & Handling: (for USA addresses)
$2.00 for first copy plus 50¢ for each additional copy

Texas residents add 8.25% sales tax

Write for a free catalog:
BIBAL Press
P.O. Box 821653
N. Richland Hills, TX 76182